T5-AGK-825

MAGNA VERITAS ET PRAEVALEBIT

Nihil obstat :

    Fr. STANISLAUS HICKEY, O.Cist.⎫
    Fr. DOMINICUS NOLAN, O.Cist. ⎬ *Censores*

Die 20ª Januarii, 1931.

Imprimatur :

    Fr. HERMANUS JOSEPH SMETS,

                  Abbas Generalis O.Cist.

Die 10ª Februarii, 1931.

Nihil obstat :

    Rev. W. A. COFFEY, *Censor.*

Imprimatur :

    ✠ BERNARDUS,

          Epus. Waterfordiensis et Lismorensis.

Waterfordiae, die 30ª Jan., 1931.

F. Armand Jeanvene: ab: de la Trappe

(At the age of 70)

THE REAL DE RANCÉ

ILLUSTRIOUS PENITENT AND REFORMER OF NOTRE DAME DE LA TRAPPE

By

AILBE J. LUDDY

O. CIST.

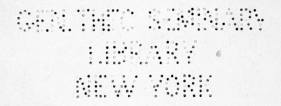
LONGMANS, GREEN AND CO.

LONDON · NEW YORK · TORONTO

1931

First published in 1931

27.125S
L965
91640

LONGMANS, GREEN AND CO. LTD.
39 PATERNOSTER ROW, LONDON, E.C.4
6 OLD COURT HOUSE STREET, CALCUTTA
53 NICOL ROAD, BOMBAY
MOUNT ROAD, MADRAS

LONGMANS, GREEN AND CO.
55 FIFTH AVENUE, NEW YORK
221 EAST 20TH STREET, CHICAGO
88 TREMONT STREET, BOSTON
128-132 UNIVERSITY AVENUE, TORONTO

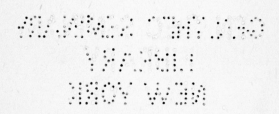

Printed in Ireland at The Talbot Press. Dublin

Reverendissimo Domino

Hermano Joseph Smets

Cistercii Archicoenobii Abbati
Necnon
Cisterciensium Strictioris Observantiae
Supremo Moderatori

Qui et Primi Trappensium Reformatoris
Partes hodie gerit

Haec Vita Armandi De Rancé
Devote inscribitur

CONTENTS

FOREWORD

About eighteen months ago an Irish prelate handed me a volume and asked me to look through it, saying that he had heard it described by a French religious as a bad book. The volume bore the title *Abbé Tempête*. It was written in a lively and entertaining style, and showed that its author, M. Henri Bremond, member of the French Academy, was a man of much literary taste and wide culture, with a special gift for satire. Before I had reached the end of the first chapter I fully understood why it was described as a bad book, and I quite agreed with the verdict. It was undoubtedly a bad book, a nasty book it has been called by a recent reviewer. Not that it contained anything opposed to Christian faith or morality—in these respects I had no fault to find with it—but because it presented to the reader as an authentic portrait of a saintly monk what was really a caricature. The *Abbé Tempête* might answer very well as a psychological novel—it is admittedly a clever piece of writing—but as a biography of the Reformer of La Trappe it can only be characterised as a travesty of truth. How anyone could seriously offer this ugly amalgam of half-truths, suspicions, insinuations, and " likely guesses " as a study of De Rancé passes comprehension.

It is not very long since an eminent artist horrified the Christian world by exhibiting a grotesque statue of the Virgin and Child. Bremond's book will produce something of the same feeling in the minds of those who see De Rancé, not through the distorting clouds of prejudice or ignorance, but as Bossuet saw him, as Mabillon saw him, as King James saw him, as he has been seen by every fair-minded man from his own to the present generation—the *saint abbé* of history and tradition.

Mr. Sheed, who has hastened to provide the English reading public with a very admirable translation of the *Abbé Tempête* under the title : *The Thundering Abbot,* considers that many other celebrities as well as De Rancé would lose their claim to esteem " if they had their Bremond." There can be no doubt of it. Bremond, with his method of criticism, could ruin any reputation. Give an artist—he need not be a very skilful one— a brush and a pot of paint and send him into the Louvre : in a very short time he will be able to convert or pervert every beautiful portrait into a hideous monstrosity. A slight touch to eye, or nose, or mouth, and the sacrilege has been perpetrated. I am quite sure that anyone malicious enough, by raking the gutter-press and keeping eyes and ears tightly closed against the *altera pars,* would succeed in making out such a character for the most exalted and respected personages in

Church and State as would qualify them for admission to the Rogues' Gallery.

The *Abbé Tempête* would rob De Rancé not alone of his reputation for virtue and sanctity, but even of his reputation for intellectual gifts. Bremond represents the illustrious Reformer as a liar, a coward, a tyrant, a hypocrite, a shallow-minded pedant intoxicated with self-conceit, who could nevertheless so impose upon the world as to be regarded as a saint and a genius. Facts are accepted, rejected, or modified, according as they help or hinder this view. The method is simplicity itself, and infallibly efficacious.

He appraises his sources by this criterion of adaptability to his end. Witnesses whose depositions are altogether favourable to De Rancé are either not cited at all or only to be turned down as " apologists," an epithet expressive of the most withering scorn on the lips of M. Bremond. They even run the risk of becoming involved in their hero's guilt if they show excessive zeal in vindicating his honour. Thus, Bossuet defends the Abbot of La Trappe against the suspicion of Jansenism. Bremond immediately points an accusing finger at the great Bishop : " Surely thou also art one of them for even thy speech doth discover thee." The Abbé Dubois has given us the fullest and best-documented *Life* of the Reformer. But Bremond has caught him in a conspiracy, a conspiracy for the canonisation of De Rancé! Worse than that, the infatuated Abbé has been discovered in an attempt to make black seem white, so that the Reformer would receive the honours of the altar not for his virtues but for his vices! Yet the Academician himself can pose as a black-and-white artist, equally skilful with the whitewash and the tar-brush. Pére Serrant writes a noble book on De Rancé and Bossuet, and in his sub-title calls the former a great monk. Bremond has not the patience to wait for more. The witness is unceremoniously turned down. Great monk, indeed!

Le Nain and the other early biographers speak in scandalised tones of the dissipated hunting-habits of the unregenerate De Rancé. Cunning rogues! Under this show of saintly simplicity a deep design is concealed. They are just making a noise about small faults to distract attention from the more serious ones on which they use the soft pedal : apologists masquerading as critics! One of these early writers meets with more courtesy than the rest. This is Dom Gervaise, who became abbot of La Trappe after De Rancé's resignation, but, being forced to resign, abandoned the monastery. He published his *Jugement critique* in 1744, that is, forty-four years after the Reformer's death. The book, with a great deal of tittle-tattle, contains much sharp criticism of Monsieur Maisne, De Rancé's secretary, whom Gervaise holds responsible for nearly all his troubles. This criticism—obviously inspired by jealousy and vindictiveness—sometimes reflects unfavourably on De Rancé himself. Hence Bremond's appreciation. But when Gervaise solemnly declares that his illustrious predecessor had never any sympathy with the systems of either Molina or Jansen, but consistently followed the guidance of St. Thomas, he is no longer considered a qualified witness. He has ceased to fit the procrustean bed.

In dealing with De Rancé directly, M. Bremond shows himself incredibly rude. Over and over again he accuses the saintly Abbot of deception. In his old age the Reformer admitted with shame and contrition that the famous Greek commentary on Anacreon was his own work. Bremond flatly contradicts him. You did *not* write it. Don't tell me. *Credat Judaeus, non ego.* You may deceive Richelieu, and Louis XIII, and Bossuet, and poor old Dubois, but you can't deceive me. That commentary is from the pen of Bellérophon.

Arnauld, Quesnel and the other Jansenistic leaders visit La Trappe and are hospitably entertained. Ha! See how this De Rancé fraternises with the enemies of the Church. " What further need have we of witnesses?" Later on, two other Jansenists arrive at the monastery, Bishop de Caulet and M Wallon. The Abbot refuses to see them himself or to allow any member of the community to see them. Bremond contemplates the scene with righteous indignation. Oh, you cruel man, is this what you call Christian charity? What harm would a little civility even towards Jansenists do to you or your religious?

The Abbot's undoubted change of manner with regard to the sectarians the critic ascribes to fear of King Louis XIV. It did not enter into his scope to explain that, after signing their submission to the Holy See and for so long as their submission could be regarded as sincere, De Rancé like Pope Clement treated the Jansenists as loyal children of the Church. It was different when their bad faith became too manifest to be any longer in doubt. No, in this matter as in many others the critic prefers to represent the Reformer as changing sides through cowardice and inconstancy, and displaying the same fanatical zeal on one side as on the other :

> " Stiff in opinion, always in the wrong,
> Everything by starts and nothing long."

M. Bremond appears to be endowed with wonderful gifts. He can read the thoughts and intents of the heart. Thus, he looks into De Rancé's mind and discovers there a very strange phenomenon : .the Abbot, it seems, has such an extraordinary mental constitution that he cannot

think at all unless he thinks *against* somebody !
Telepathy is another of his gifts. He can repro-
duce a conversation carried on between De Rancé
and his Jansenistic visitors, of which, as he con-
fesses, absolutely no record remains. More amazing
still, the limitless range of his knowledge includes
even the pure *futurabilia,* the things that would be
done, freely yet infallibly, positing a certain condition, but actually will never be, because that
condition has not been posited. Hitherto that kind
of knowledge was supposed to be a divine pre-
rogative. But M. Henri Bremond can inform us
what course things would have taken at Port Royal
had De Rancé become a Jansenist. Assuredly, it
was not for nothing our critic was made a member of
the French Academy.

But people who show themselves so commendably
zealous for the truth and so severe against violators
—real or supposed—of veracity, should be careful
not to indulge in " mountainous exaggerations," to
borrow Mr. Chesterton's phrase. To say, as
Bremond does, that the Abbot of La Trappe spent
the best part of his life after his ordination abusing
the Jesuits, is quite Himalayan hyperbole. And
what are we to think of Father de la Chaise, S.J.,
who was the eulogist and defender of this intran-
sigent opponent of the Society ? He says also that
no sane person would prefer De Rancé to
Bourdaloue as spiritual director. For the honour

of seventeenth-century France, I sincerely hope
he is mistaken. I simply refuse to believe that the
multitude of people, including cardinals, bishops,
members of *la haute noblesse,* and " monks and
nuns of divers Orders," who *did* prefer De Rancé
were all mentally unsound. How different Bossuet's
estimate ! According to the great Bishop of Meaux,
Abbot de Rancé was " the most perfect director
of souls in the monastic life that the world has
seen since the immortal Abbot of Clairvaux."[1]

To the accusations of pharisaical pride and
contempt of others, De Rancé might answer in the
words used by St. Bernard in reply to *his*—an
infinitely superior—Bremond : " If this be true, to
what purpose ' are we killed all the day long and
counted as sheep for the slaughter ' ? If thus, I
say, with pharisaical arrogance we despise other
men and our betters, what avails the poverty of
our dress, the coarseness and scantiness of our
food, our hard and uninterrupted labour, our
constant fastings and watchings, in a word, all
the austerities of our life ?

" Do we suffer all this to be seen and admired of
men ? Then shall we deserve that Christ should
say of us : ' They have received their reward '
(Matt. vi, 3). Surely, ' if in this life only we have
hope in Christ, we are of all men the most miserable'

---

[1] " *Le plus parfait directeur des âmes dans la vie monastique qu'on eût connu depuis l'immortel abbé de Clairvaux.*"

(1 Cor. xv, 19).   But what hope can we have in
Him beyond the present life, if in His service we
seek after temporal glory ? Alas for us, who endure
so much labour and pain in order to appear different
from other men, meriting thereby a more awful
damnation !   Surely we might have found an easier
road to hell !   If we are determined to enter that
region of woe, why did we not at least choose the
broad and pleasant way in which many walk to
perdition ?   Why not a gay instead of a gloomy
passage to death ? Oh, how much happier the lot
of those who abandon themselves to the pleasures
of life, ' who have no part in the labours of men,
neither are they scourged like other men ' (Ps.
lxxii. 5), who, sinners though they are and destined
to feed the everlasting fires, nevertheless enjoy here
a short period of bliss and prosperity ! Woe to him
who bears a cross that is not, like the Saviour's,
fruitful of good, but unprofitable to himself like
that of Simon the Cyrenian ! Woe to the harpers
that play not on their own harps, as those
mentioned in the Apocalypse (xiv, 2), but, as
hypocrites, on the harps of others ! Woe, double
woe to them who bear the cross of Christ indeed,
yet not in the following of Christ, who share in
His Passion but have no part in His humility !''

The above would well describe the position of
De Rancé were he such as his critic represents him

to have been. His conversion would have made a
libertine the less and a hypocrite the more, who
could look for no reward in the future life and certainly did not receive much in the present : for even
Bremond has not the hardihood to maintain that
the Abbot performed *all* his penance by proxy. But
the *Abbé Tempête* has nothing in common with the
venerable Abbot of La Trappe ; it is the monstrous
product of a fertile imagination and may end, as
Frankenstein's monster ended, in destroying its
creator.

Somewhere in his book M. Bremond acknowledges that he has a strong taste for comedy. That,
I am willing to allow, is an extenuating circumstance. Comedians are a privileged class. The
Knight of the Cap and Bells has his uses. In these
dull dyspeptic days he helps to brighten the dreary
hours and to keep us in good humour. If people
laugh at his jokes and fling him a copper, that is
his luck. Nobody can reasonably object to it. It
is only when he forgets his rôle and takes himself
seriously and assumes pontifical airs that one feels
tempted to disregard his privilege and administer
the knout.

Finally, without any pretensions to prophetic
gifts, I will venture to promise M. Bremond that
De Rancé's books, for which he professes so much
contempt, will continue to be read and admired
when the *Abbé Tempête* will have gone the way

of all rubbish, and that the illustrious Abbot will live for ever in the hearts of his grateful disciples as an ideal and an inspiration, despite all the efforts of maligners, be they French Academicians or run-away monks.

MOUNT MELLERAY,
December 29th, 1930.

THE REAL DE RANCÉ

CHAPTER I.

Pedigree — Birth — Early Education — Death of Denis-François — Tonsured — Ecclesiastical Dignities — Commendatory Abbots — First Examination.

UNLIKE their Anglo-Irish namesakes, the French Bouthilliers were not a fighting race. They appear to have preferred the peaceful practice of the law to the profession of arms. Nevertheless, they came of Celtic stock, for the best authorities assure us that Brittany was their homeland. Yet it was not from Brittany they came to the capital, but from Angoulême, where they had resided during several generations, and held offices of some importance. So far, they were just a respectable bourgeois family with no particular claims to distinction. None of the name figured very prominently in the history of France, at least not until the last quarter of the sixteenth century. At that time the real founder of the family, Denis le Bouthillier, appeared in Paris, where he soon made himself known as a legist of extraordinary ability, profoundly versed both in ecclesiastical and civil law. His house, so

1

we are informed, became the rendezvous of church-men of all grades, who came to consult him about their legal difficulties. He does not seem to have been a very ambitious man, for he refused the important post of advocate-general to the Parliament, offered him by Henry III.

In the year 1576 he married one Claudine Machesco who bore him nine children : five girls of whom all but one entered religion, and four boys. The eldest son, Claude, became Superintendent of Finance, and received the title of Marquis de Pons-sur-Seine ; from him derived the noble families of Bouthillier de Chavigny, and Bouthillier de Beaujeu. Sebastian and Victor took orders, and both were advanced to the episcopate, the former being ap-pointed Bishop of Aire, the latter Archbishop of Tours. Nor did the youngest, named Denis after his father, lag behind his brothers in the race for honours. He became private secretary to the Queen-Mother, Marie de Médicis, president of the *chambre des comptes,* royal counsellor, treasurer, keeper of the seal, etc. He married a lady named Charlotte Joly, daughter of an eminent lawyer who held the position of chief counsellor to Cardinal Richelieu, Minister of State and virtual sovereign. Of this union eight children were born, three boys and five girls. Three of the girls became religieuses : Françoise and Marie-Louise entered the Annonciades in Paris, and Thérèse went to the Clairets, the name given to a community of Cistercian nuns in the diocese of Chartres. Claude-Catherine married twice, first Count de Belin, then Count d'Albon. Marie espoused the Lord of Roche-Vernassal, and by him became the mother of a very distinguished soldier.

The eldest boy, Denis-François, was intended for the Church. He was the protégé of his uncle, the Bishop of Aire. Philip-Charles, the youngest entered the navy, where he rose to the rank of admiral.

But it is with the second son of Denis le Bouthillier we are particularly concerned. He was born in Paris on January 9th, 1626. Very special pains were taken to propitiate the goddess fortune in his regard. Richelieu himself, the all-powerful Cardinal-Minister, acted as godfather, and gave the child his own name : Armand-Jean. The place of godmother was assigned to another illustrious personage, the Marchioness d'Effiat, wife of the Superintendent of Finance. Young Armand-Jean le Bouthillier de Rancé—the father had made the addition to the surname after his marriage in order to distinguish his own from the other branches of the family—undoubtedly began his career under favourable auspices. Was anything more required to place his future beyond hazard ? Yes, he needed to have brains. Without that endowment, powerful patronage would avail him little or nothing. But in this respect, at all events, young Bouthillier did not disappoint his patrons. As he grew up he gave proof of astonishing precociousness. This delighted beyond measure his worldly father, a veritable slave to greed and ambition. Obsessed with an unholy desire to see his family advancing in wealth, power, and dignity, he was not at all over-scrupulous as to the means he employed for attaining his end.

As it had been decided to spare no expense in Armand-Jean's education, two private tutors of note were charged with the direction of his classical studies—M. de Bellérophon for Greek, and the Abbé Favier for Latin. They had every reason to be proud of their pupil's progress, for he acquired a wonderful mastery of both languages ; nor, as we shall see, did he ever forget the devotion of his early teachers.

The ambition of the Bouthillier family suffered a serious check by the disgrace of the Queen-Mother, Marie de Médicis, in February 1631. She had made quite a pet of Armand-Jean, her "little Ranqué," as she used to call him, and was often seen with that *enfant terrible* on her lap. But with his godfather, the Cardinal-Minister, she did not get on quite so well. Richelieu complained of her influence with the King, and one day informed Louis XIII that he must make choice between the Queen-Mother and his Prime Minister, because the Court had not capacity to contain the two. The Monarch chose the Minister. Marie de Médicis was forced to taste the bitterness of an exile's lot. Of course, the Queen-Mother's trusted secretary participated in her disgrace. He was made to feel distinctly that he no longer enjoyed Richelieu's favour, and did not venture thereafter to present himself at court.

But the Cardinal-Minister did not penalise the other members of the family. It was whilst the weight of his displeasure rested upon Denis that he appointed his brother, Claude le Bouthillier, Super-intendent of Finance, and Claude's son, a young man of twenty-six, Secretary of State. About the same time he named Anne-Marie, Denis's eldest sister, Lady Abbess of the convent of Saint-Antoine in Paris. Ill-natured people suspected that Richelieu's object in thus showering honours and dignities on poor Denis's relatives was just to excite his envy.

When Armand-Jean was in his tenth year, his elder brother Denis-François, fell seriously ill. It soon became manifest that nothing short of a miracle would save the lad, but, alas! such a supernatural interposition could hardly be expected in a house-hold so worldly as that of Denis le Bouthillier. We have called Denis-François a lad, for such he was in years; but judged according to his dignities, the term sounds irreverent, almost sacrilegious. For he had already acquired, through the favour of influential friends, a large number of ecclesiastical titles and

benefices ; he was a canon of Notre Dame, Paris ;
abbot of the Cistercian monastery of Notre Dame
de la Trappe, abbot of the Benedictine monastery
of Saint-Symphorien de Beauvais, abbot of the
Augustinian monastery of Notre Dame du Val,
prior of the Grandmontine monastery near Boulogne, and almoner to the King. The revenues
from all amounted to something like 15,000 livres,
or about £750 per annum. Not bad for a beginning.

In the sorrow that overwhelmed him at the
prospect of losing his son, M. Denis did not forget
the financial aspects of that loss, and took timely
precautions to preserve all the benefices in his
family. He caused Armand-Jean, whom he had
hitherto destined for the army, to be tonsured and
so qualified to acquire and to hold the property of
the Church. The dying youth then transferred to
his younger brother all the honours and emoluments
he was possessed of, with the exception of the
canonry of Notre Dame. To obtain that a little
more time and a little—very little—more ceremony
would be needed.

Denis-François had a long illness. He died on
September 17th, 1637. On the 19th, the day
after the funeral, M. Denis le Bouthillier conducted
his second son, Armand-Jean, to the cathedral of
Notre Dame, and presented to the chapter letters
from the Archbishop of Paris transferring the

canonry and prebend possessed by the late Denis-
François to his younger brother, who was a clerk of
the metropolitan church. The boy took the usual
oath, then vested in his canonical robes, was installed with due solemnity. He thus became at the
age of eleven and a half a member of that venerable
senate which ruled the primatial diocese. Remember
he had already been an abbot, nay, a manifold
abbot for eighteen months ; and surely an abbot
at ten may very well become a canon at eleven.
As some of his colleagues were no older than
himself, he did not want for playmates in the
chapter. Of course, these young canons were dis-
pensed from the obligation of attending choir or
reciting the canonical office. The indulgent
authorities required no more from them than that
they should assist at High Mass and receive Holy
Communion in the cathedral on the four principal
festivals of the year. But even that modicum of
service was considered too much for Armand-Jean
le Bouthillier, so his father asked and obtained for
him a dispensation from the public Communions on
the score of weak health. Needless to say, the
delicacy which prevented him from discharging the
light duties attaching to his benefice did not by any
means prevent his appropriating the revenues thereof.

Readers unfamiliar with monastic history will
wonder to hear of children being appointed abbots.

The title of abbot to their minds belongs only to one who governs a monastery, observing the monastic rule himself and seeing that it is observed by those under his charge. How is it possible, they will ask, for a boy of ten to do this? But they need not be uneasy. The baby-abbot had even less responsibility than the baby-canon. Armand-Jean was not a regular abbot—that would imply profession in the Order and residence in the house— but what is known as a commendatory abbot. A commendatory abbot, *abbas in commendam,* is any person, ecclesiastical or lay, entitled to draw the revenues of a monastery without any responsibility whatsoever with regard to the discipline of the house. We first meet with such abbots in the pontificate of Pope Gregory the Great (590—604), who sometimes handed over the revenues of vacant abbeys for the support of bishops exiled from their sees. Other Pontiffs followed this example. Later on, the civil rulers claimed the same right as the Popes to make such appointments, and, needless to say, the good of the monasteries and the interests of religion were usually the least of their concerns. In the year 1122 Pope Calixtus II forbade the appointment of laymen as commendatory abbots; but at the commencement of the fourteenth century the evil broke out again and made the Cistercian Order its particular prey.

The right of free election practically ceased to

exist. Profligate kings saw nothing incongruous in making presents of rich abbeys to their favourites, with a fine impartiality as to character, age, even sex and religion. There have been commendatory abbots seven years old. Henry IV of France presented an abbey to the Countess of Guiche, and another to the Protestant Rosny. In the same kingdom where the crown had an unlimited right of nomination, nearly all the Cistercian houses, including Citeaux itself, came to be held *in commendam*. The situation was nearly as bad in the other countries of Europe, not excepting England and Scotland. Is it necessary to remark that these nominal abbots stripped their monasteries bare, and often enough left the monks without the means of subsistence? It was simply useless to protest against the scandalous disorder, for there appeared to be no power on earth strong enough to cope with it. In 1473 the Cistercian General Chapter sent a deputation to Rome, entreating Sixtus IV to put an end once and for all to the bad institution. The account given by the deputies of the sad condition to which the commendatory abbots had reduced their Order moved the Pope and cardinals to tears. Nevertheless the Holy See found itself powerless to provide a remedy. The evil was too widespread and deep-rooted, and for once '' there was no balm in Galaad.''

Madame de Rancé died October 14th, 1638.

Very unlike her husband, she seems to have been more concerned for her children's spiritual welfare than for their worldly prosperity. Armand-Jean was the object of her special solicitude and the child of her heart. He, on his side, fully reciprocated her affection. During her last illness, he could hardly be induced to leave her bedside, and his only consolation was to minister to her wants. She was buried in the church of the Discalced Carmelites, Rue de Vaugirard, which she and her husband had chosen as their last resting-place.

It was an unspeakable misfortune for Armand-Jean to have lost this good mother just at the time when he needed her most. How different his career might have been had she survived to guide his footsteps through the critical period on which he was about to enter ! However, Providence had its own designs. If he was to have no Monica on earth to pursue him with her prayers in his wanderings, he would have his Monica in heaven.

Meantime, the Queen, Anne of Austria, had received M. de Rancé into favour, and brought his eldest daughter, Claude-Catherine, to court as maid of honour. But he had not yet succeeded in regaining the Cardinal-Minister's goodwill, which was absolutely essential to his hopes. For neither King nor Queen would have the temerity to advance one who had the misfortune to incur Richelieu's displeasure, at least before reconciliation. Good-bye, therefore, to all prospect of promotion if the present state of things continued. But what was to be done? A plan suggested itself. The Cardinal was well known as a patron of learning. He could admire talent even in an opponent, as he proved in the case of the Abbé St. Cyran. Perhaps he could be approached with success on that side. So Armand-Jean was set to work on a critical edition of the Greek lyric poet, Anacreon. The result appeared in due time with a Greek commentary and a dedicatory epistle, in elegant Latin, to the Cardinal-Minister. How much of this work the brilliant pupil could justly claim as his own composition and how much, if any, must be credited to his master, M. Bellerophon, it is impossible to decide. Different biographers take different views. M. Bremond, of course, adopts the opinion least honourable to Armand-Jean. However, young De Rancé's reputation for scholarship rests on a firmer foundation than is afforded by his edition of Anacreon.

The plan succeeded. Richelieu put aside his resentment and promised to recompense the young author with another benefice, richer than any of those he already possessed. Father Caussin, S.J., confessor to the King, vehemently protested against this accumulation of ecclesiastical revenues in the

---

[1] In a letter written in the sixty-eighth year of his age, De Rancé testifies that the Greek commentary was his own work; *cf.* Dubois, *Histoire de l'Abbé de Rancé,* I., 26. But, of course, M. Bremond knows better.

hands of a child : Armand-Jean had not yet entered upon his teens. " God grant I may never bestow benefices on less worthy subjects," replied Louis. " Why, this youngster knows more Greek and Latin than any abbé in my kingdom."

The good Jesuit, however, remained unconvinced. He decided to subject this much-admired but probably over-estimated youngster to the test of a strict examination. So he sent for De Rancé without giving him any warning of the ordeal in store. As soon as the boy arrived, he was presented with an open Homer, and asked to translate. Without a moment's hesitation he rendered into fluent French the passage indicated. Father Caussin, suspecting that he derived some help from the Latin translation printed on the same page, covered the Latin with a glove. Armand-Jean appeared not to notice his action. He read on without interruption. Even M. Bremond does not suggest that there might have been a hole in the glove. The Jesuit realised his mistake ; this boy did in truth deserve his reputation. Unable to conceal his admiration he cried out with enthusiasm : " You have the eyes of a lynx, but sharper still is your intellect." There was no further opposition to his getting the benefice.

CHAPTER II.

*Harcourt—Affection for Tutors—Richelieu dies—
Armand-Jean a Master in Arts—Theological
Student—Baccalaureate in Sacred Theology—
First Sermon — Pastimes — Companions — Per-
sonal Appearance.*

IN the year of grace 1642, the seventeenth of his
age, Armand-Jean entered the college of Harcourt,
Rue de la Harpe, Paris, to begin his philosophical
studies. It grieved him to part with his beloved
tutors, MM. Favier and Bellerophon, and he
declared he would never forget them, never cease
to regard them as his kind and patient benefactors.
We might have anticipated it would be so with De
Rancé, for gratitude is always the characteristic
of noble natures. The affection he entertained for
these humble scholars is to our mind one of the
most beautiful traits in his beautiful character. He
never ceased to interest himself in their concerns
and to correspond with them, even at a time when
the world's greatest and noblest prided themselves
on being his friends. " I leave you to judge," he
wrote, complainingly, to Favier, " whether or not
I have just cause to reproach you and to suspect

that you account me unworthy of your letters : for I have four times written to you without once getting a reply." Again : " Your last letter filled me with joy and happiness. I am delighted beyond expression to know that you still entertain so much affection for me. For myself, I am yours entirely and for ever." To M. Bellerophon : " My first act on receiving your letter was to press it to my lips, since I could not enjoy the happiness of embracing the writer . . . . As ingratitude is a crime I can never be guilty of, I must forget myself before I can forget my obligations to you." " I am very sorry to hear of your illness, both on account of your present suffering and on account of what is to come. However, as the malady has not yet taken deep root, you must employ every means in your power to arrest its progress. Do this, I conjure you by the interest I take in your health. You know how precious it is to me both for your sake and for my own." And in his sixty-seventh year, when worn out with toil and penance, and scarcely able to hold the pen, he wrote from his comfortless cell to his old Greek master, then bowed beneath the weight of four score years and three : " I thank God for having preserved your life so long. I ask Him in fervent prayer to prolong it still more, and to fill you with happiness. Never cease, I beg of you, to keep me in your love. As for me, I am yours *in aeternum et ultra,* with sentiments of affection which words cannot express.''

How many pupils in modern times treat their early teachers with the like consideration? But we must not attempt to canonise De Rancé, lest we should draw down upon our heads the vengeance of M. Bremond, the unofficial Devil's Advocate in the case against the Reformer of La Trappe.

At Harcourt Armand-Jean became an enthusiastic Aristotelian. The study of the Stagirite's treatise *de Coelo* led him to believe that the destinies of men are absolutely predetermined by the movements of the heavenly bodies, and may consequently be read therein. This astrological superstition had then numerous adherents amongst the French aristo-cracy, including Marie de Médicis and Anne of Austria. It was another of the many points of parallelism between De Rancé and St. Augustine ; for astrology had also fascinated for a while the mind of the Penitent-Bishop. Astrology was not the only folly our student learned at Harcourt. He became likewise a convinced alchemist, and enter-tained the wild hope of one day discovering the philosopher's stone.

1642 proved to be a calamitous year for Armand-Jean and his relatives. The sun of their prosperity seemed at last to have crossed the zenith. On December 4th, Cardinal Richelieu breathed his last. All the different branches of the Bouthillier family, we are informed, lamented the great Minister's death as almost a domestic bereavement. We can well believe it. For was it not to his patronage they were indebted for all they actually possessed of riches, power and dignities, and for all their hopes of future advancement? To Armand-Jean, in particular, the loss was truly an irreparable one. He had occupied, as he well knew, a large place in the affections of the Cardinal. Gifted as he was, and supported by such a patron, there was no eminence, however exalted, in Church or State to which he might not reasonably aspire. Now he would have to depend upon his own efforts in the struggle against fortune. It even seemed as if he would be heavily handicapped. The new Prime Minister, Cardinal Mazarin, did not look with a favourable eye upon the Bouthilliers. He dismissed Claude, Marquis de Pons-sur-Seine, from his position as Superintendent of Finance, and banished him from the capital. Claude's son, Leo, who filled the office of Secretary of State, was obliged to hand in his resignation. Evidently there was nothing to expect from the liberality of Cardinal Mazarin.

The very next day after Cardinal Richelieu's funeral, Armand-Jean had to endure another and more personal bereavement. His brother-in-law, the young Count de Belin, to whom he seems to have been warmly attached, met his death at the hand of a cowardly assassin. " But for the profession to which I belong," wrote our student-Abbé to Favier, " I should consider myself unworthy to live if I did not avenge his murder." Not very edifying language from an aspirant to the priesthood, you will say. Granted. But it shows, at all events, that he felt he owed something to his character as an ecclesiastic. If only he could have always sustained himself at that height of perfection !

Meantime, he continued his studies at Harcourt. Although, as we have seen, he dabbled a good deal in the occult sciences, he did not neglect the ordinary routine work. At the end of the first year's philosophy course, that is, in the summer of 1643, he would have to make what is called a public defension—*viz.*, to defend a philosophical thesis in public against objectors from all sides. This was the first step towards the degree of Master in Arts. He dedicated his thesis to the Queen, Anne of Austria, now Regent of France—Louis XIII having died May 14th of this year—and invited her to attend the contest. The dedication was graciously accepted ; the Queen regretted she could not witness the intellectual tournament herself, but promised to send a representative. A great throng of professors and students from all the schools in Paris assembled at Harcourt on the appointed day. Armand-Jean had no difficulty in solving the objections proposed to him, with the exception of one. A certain doctor endeavoured to drive him into a dilemma where he would have no alternative except either to abandon his position or to acknowledge himself opposed to Aristotle. Either of these courses would be as fatal as the other. The young defendant would take neither. " I have read Aristotle through," he said, " and I cannot remember to have found such an opinion expressed anywhere in his writings." The objector insisted that the opinion in question was held by the Stagirite. De Rancé challenged him to produce the text. Then it transpired that the doctor, not knowing the Greek language, had derived his objection from a faulty Latin translation. This discomfiture of one of their number angered the other objectors; they surrounded the candidate and raised such an uproar that the Duke de Montbazan, who presided, as governor of Paris, felt obliged to interfere, and drove them off with his cane. The following summer Armand-Jean made his second defension with equal éclat, and received the cap and gown of Master in Arts.

Having completed his philosophical course, it remained for Armand-Jean to begin the study of Sacred Theology. But it was decided that he should not attend the public lectures at the University of Paris, known as the Sorbonne. Instead, two of the professors would come daily to his home, one in the morning and the other in the afternoon, to read with him the scholastic authors. The reason of this arrangement we do not know. Abbé Dubois explains it by saying that the boy's father had become concerned for his spiritual welfare and feared to expose him to the many temptations of university life. We sincerely hope his explanation is the right one, but we find it somewhat difficult to visualise Denis le Bouthillier de Rancé '' among the prophets.''

Armand-Jean threw himself with enthusiasm into the study of the sacred sciences. He seems to have taken particular delight in '' making up '' the different controverted questions in theology, for he loved debate. And everything came so easy to him. He had been scarcely three months at work when he gravely informed a friend that he hoped to become a great theologian in a very short time ! He has already made up his mind as to the merits of the scholastic doctors. His admiration for St. Augustine is unbounded ; he intends to follow that holy Bishop's guidance in questions concerning grace. St. Thomas has his points, too, but his Latin is deplorable. He can hardly bring himself to read his works, and his aversion to his style has prejudiced his mind against the Saint's opinions. Remember we are listening to a youth of eighteen, a youth all whose antecedents had been eminently well qualified to foster sentiments of self-conceit. Before very long he will have revised his estimate of the Prince of theologians, and we shall hear him proclaiming that he has taken the Angelic Doctor for his guide in all matters theological.

In February, 1647, De Rancé would have to make another public defension for the degree of Baccalaureate in Sacred Theology. On the 3rd of June preceding he had to stand a preliminary examination on the doctrine of St. Thomas. For three and a half hours he was plied with questions by four learned doctors who endeavoured particularly to discover his views on grace. " I answered their questions," writes the examinee, "in such a manner as to leave them still uncertain what my opinions are." His Baccalaureate thesis also he dedicated to the Queen. During the defension he overwhelmed the objectors with his varied erudition, especially with his citations from the Fathers of the Church. It was another triumph.

Being now a Bachelor in theology, De Rancé thought it was high time to test his powers as a preacher. The necessary authorisation was easily obtained from the Archbishop of Paris. He preached his first sermon at the Annonciades on the occasion of his sister's profession. His next appearance in the pulpit was on January 25th of the following year, 1648, the feast of the Conversion of St. Paul, when he delivered a discourse of wonderful power and beauty in a church dedicated to the Doctor of

Nations. Thereafter the young pulpit orator was much in request with the faithful of the capital.

Preaching, however, was not his only recreation at this time. He also devoted much of his leisure to hunting : his leisure, unfortunately, included a great part of every day, for the extraordinary quickness of his intellect enabled him to get through his academical work with wonderful rapidity. One of his biographers assures us that sometimes " after spending three or four hours of the morning hunting, he would ride the same day twelve or fifteen leagues in order to maintain a thesis at the university or to preach in one of the city churches : and in the lecture hall or in the pulpit he would appear as calm and recollected as if he had come straight from his study." By dint of practice he became a superb and a most daring horseman. Fencing was another art that engaged his attention. He loved it for its exciting swiftness of cut, thrust, and parry, and for the analogy it bore to his pet art of disputation.

Of his companions in these sports and pastimes we know the names of four, as brilliant almost and certainly as pleasure-loving as himself. These were Etienne le Camus (later Bishop of Grenoble and Cardinal), François de Champvallon, François de Harlay (the future Archbishop of Paris), and François de Clermont-Tonnerre (the future Bishop of Noyon). They remained his friends all through life. De Champvallon, so we read, met De Rancé early one morning in the street and asked what was his programme for the day. " I shall preach like an angel in the forenoon," was the reply, " and hunt like the devil in the evening." On another occasion, De Rancé, De Clermont-Tonnerre, and De Champvallon, were discussing the torments endured by the Christian martyrs, especially the sufferings of St. Laurence. De Rancé proposed that they should try which of them would hold his finger in a candle flame the longest. His two companions made the experiment first; they could hardly support the pain an instant. Then his turn came. He bore the agony so long that the others, fearing he would be seriously burned, blew out the candle.

With regard to his personal appearance during these unregenerate years, we have the following description of him from the pen of a contemporary : " He wore a tight-fitting coat of beautiful violet-coloured material. His hair hung down his back and shoulders in long curls. He displayed two emeralds at the joining of his ruffles, and on his finger a large and costly diamond ring. When in the country indulging in the pleasures of the chase, he usually laid aside every mark of his clerical calling, carried a sword at his side and a brace of pistols in his holsters. His dress now was fawn-coloured, and he used to wear a black cravat embroidered with gold. In the more serious society, wherein he was occasionally compelled to mix, he considered himself very clerical indeed when he put on a coat of black velvet with buttons of gold.'' When we add to this that he had a perfect figure, tall, slim, and upright, every movement marked with exquisite grace : that his face was strikingly handsome : a lofty forehead, large, lustrous eyes, a straight, prominent nose, a beautifully formed but firm mouth, with a complexion still delicately-tinted despite so much outdoor exercise ; that in charm of manner and brilliancy of conversational powers he had few equals even amongst the Parisians of that polished generation, the reader will have some idea of the young Abbé De Rancé as he appeared to his contemporaries, and will understand why he was such a favourite everywhere and a welcome guest at the noblest houses of the capital.

CHAPTER III.

Ordained Priest—Licentiate in Theology—Death of M. Denis de Rancé—Doctor in Theology— Worldliness—De Rancé as a Pulpit Orator— Veretz—Narrow Escape from Death.

ARMAND-JEAN was perfectly satisfied with the manner of life he had been hitherto leading : brilliant academical triumphs alternating with the exciting pleasures of the chase and the fencing-school and the gaming-table and the gentler pleasures of the ballroom : for, truth to tell, our young Abbé had become quite a society man, in the fullest sense of the term. This kind of existence suited him, and he wanted no change. Above all, he wanted to enter the Sanctuary no further than he had already gone. If he had submitted to the ceremony of tonsure, it was because, on the one hand, that was an essential qualification for the receiving and holding of ecclesiastical benefices, and, on the other, it imposed no galling restraints upon his liberty ; in other words, it conferred upon him what he considered the benefits of the clerical state without any of its burdens. But the case would be altogether different if he took Holy Orders, there-

24

fore no Holy Orders for him. But then there was his uncle Victor, Archbishop of Tours, clamouring to have him for coadjutor, of course with the right of succession. And just now his Grace was reported seriously ill. If he should happen to die before his nephew's ordination, gone perhaps for ever would be our Abbé's chance of a mitre, at least so long as episcopal nominations remained in Mazarin's gift. M. Denis de Rancé represented the situation in all its seriousness to his dutiful son. It took a good deal of talking, and perhaps a few tears to overcome his reluctance. Even then he did not give way entirely : the matter ended in a compromise. He promised to go as far as the Diaconate imme-diately ; then he would pause awhile to take breath. It was a pity Tours lay at so great a distance from his beloved Paris. But after all, the archiepiscopal dignity was well worth making some sacrifice to attain. Yes, he would become a priest. But he wanted a little time for reflection before taking the final step.

A dispensation from the canonical interstices permitted him to receive the four Minor Orders, Subdiaconate and Diaconate on three consecutive days of December, 1648. He prepared for the solemn ceremony by making a retreat of twelve days at the Vincentian house of St. Lazarus, under the direction of St. Vincent de Paul himself. During this time of fervour, the holy director took the opportunity to represent to him the wrongfulness of holding so many benefices, and begged him to be satisfied with one, as the sacred canons allowed no more. "Reverend Father," answered the retreatant, "will you please postpone your recommendations on this subject until another time? The question is new to me, and I must examine it before I can come to any decision." However, he agreed to have his hair cut short, and to dress in a manner somewhat more in keeping with his calling. The ordaining prelate was Jean-François-Paul de Gondi, then coadjutor Archbishop of Paris, afterwards better known as Cardinal de Retz.

Soon after the ceremony Armand-Jean wrote to his friend Favier: "You have formed too good an opinion of my vocation to the ecclesiastical state. Provided it has been according to the Will of God, I am quite content; for as Christians, we ought not to have any thought or intention save such as He approves." Very edifying sentiments these. If only they were lasting! But although the hair will not be permitted any more to grow long and curl, although for the future he will look a little less like a cavalier and a little more like a cleric, the old passions will again revive. Much water must yet flow down the Seine to the sea before Armand-Jean is converted in earnest.

His ordination to the priesthood took place on January 22nd, 1651, when he was entering on the

twenty-sixth year of his age. His uncle, the Archbishop, journeyed from Tours to Paris to officiate
on the occasion ; nor did he show any clear signs
of approaching dissolution. So there had been no
need of hurry after all. Armand-Jean must have
congratulated himself on having had the good
sense to wait. He had thereby gained two full
years. After the ordination he disappeared from
Paris, to the wonder and consternation of his friends.
Their wonder was not lessened when it transpired
that he had actually shut himself up in a Carthusian
monastery where he was devoting all his time to
prayer. His good father must have got a bad fright.
A priest on the way to an archbishopric was one
thing, a priest confined for life to a monastic cell
was quite another. However, there was no occasion
for uneasiness. The neophyte reappeared after a
few days : he had only gone to make a retreat. He
said his first Mass in the church where he had
preached his first sermon.

In the spring of the following year (1652) our
Abbé stood his final examination for the degree of
Licentiate in Theology. That distinction was not
so easy to win then as it is now. The ordeal in
question—the last of many and called the Sor-
bonique—lasted from 6 a.m. to 6 p.m. For twelve
consecutive hours the candidate was kept under fire,
endeavouring to answer difficulties proposed by the
subtlest minds in Paris. There was always fierce

rivalry amongst both students and professors. Happy
the candidate whose name came first in the order of
merit, and happy the professor who could claim him
as his pupil !   Amongst those competing with De
Rancé was Jacques Benignus Bossuet, later to be
called the Eagle of Meaux.   Although rivals now,
the two were close friends, and friends they would
remain until death parted them.   They had much
in common ; both had been precocious prodigies,
both had acquired immense erudition, both were
endowed with extraordinary powers of eloquence.
But there was also much in which they differed ;
Bossuet was always grave, pious, and diligent,
whereas his friend, although perhaps pious by fits
and starts, had never been remarkable for either
diligence or gravity.

It belonged to the principal doctors of the
Sorbonne, assembled in secret session, to determine
the order of merit after the final ordeal.   The
results were announced on the Monday preceding
Ash Wednesday, in the Archbishop's chapel, as
custom required.   The list of names may still be
seen as entered in the university register.   It runs
as follows :

1. Magister Joannes Arm. le Bouthillier,
   canon., Paris.

2. Magister Gasto Chamillard, Sorbon., Prior.

3. Magister Jacob Benignus Bossuet, Navar.

4. Magister Nicolaus de la Haye, Sorbon., Prior.

5. Magister Jacobus de Mailly, Sorb., etc.

People have been surprised that Bossuet got only third place, and different explanations have been offered. Bremond, with his customary cocksureness, accuses the judges of favouritism. De Rancé came first, not through merit—merit indeed ! how could one disliked by M. Henri Bremond possess any merit ?—but because of his standing at court. Chamillard came second, because he was a high official of the university. Then Bossuet, because he had most knowledge. Perhaps he had. It seems to us, however, that the fault of the judges—the venerable heads of the first university in Europe—was not, in Bremond's eyes, to have put Bossuet third, but rather to have put De Rancé first. Bremond is not in the least concerned for the honour of Bossuet, but he is very much concerned to see that De Rancé is kept down. As for our Abbé's standing at court, there must be a blunder here. At this particular time his family were anything but in favour. His uncle, Claude Bouthillier, had been disgraced by the Cardinal-Minister. His cousin, Leo, after resigning his office as Secretary of State, had been arrested on the charge of having been implicated in the conspiracy known as the

Fronde,[1] and still languished in prison. His father, who had served the State so long and so loyally, was left without any employment. It is really hard to see what the Sorbonne examiners had to gain by giving Armand-Jean an honour he did not deserve, even if they were as dishonest as M. Bremond supposes them to have been.

M. Denis le Bouthillier de Rancé, if not as wealthy as he would have wished to be, was nevertheless by no means what we should call a poor man. Besides two splendid mansions in the capital, he possessed a fine estate and a beautiful country residence at Veretz in Touraine. He happened to be staying at this rustic seat in February, 1654, superintending some improvements, when he was suddenly attacked by the illness which proved to be his last. Armand-Jean was summoned in hot haste from Paris. On his arrival he found the old man in a dying condition ; he had made his peace with God, and showed more of the Christian spirit at the hour of death than might have been expected from a man of his habits and character. He bequeathed to his son, the Abbé, two legacies : one

---

1 That is, the new Fronde, led by the Duke of Orleans and Prince de Condé. It was an effort on the part of the nobles to get rid of Mazarin whom they regarded as an unscrupulous tyrant. The army of the Fronde suffered a final defeat near Paris in 1652. There can be no doubt that the Abbé de Rancé's relatives took an important part in the conspiracy. He himself was accused of writing seditious pamphlets over the signature of Cardinal de Retz.

was the moral counsel to put honour and conscience before all other interests, the other, less spiritual but we fear not less appreciated by the legatee, the whole of his earthly possessions. It was his wish to be buried beside his wife in the church of the Discalced Carmelites. So, thither he came to repose at last after his life-long and wearisome pursuit of fortune.

Hardly had his respected father been laid in the grave when Armand-Jean was called upon to make his defension for the degree of Doctor in Theology. In spite of the loss of time and the many distractions during the past year, he sustained his thesis with brilliant success, and was voted to have won the doctorate. The question whether he should present himself for the decorations in his academical or in his canonical robes gave rise to a warm dispute between the university authorities and the chapter of Notre Dame. The latter body was obliged to give way.

We have now arrived at the most critical period of our Abbé's career. He was still a young man, in the twenty-eighth year of his age, rich—his total income came to about one million francs (present value) per annum—handsome, learned, honoured, complete master of his time, and having the entrée to the proudest families and the most exclusive circles in Paris. His father, whilst he lived, had

exercised some restraining influence on him. Not
that M. Denis troubled himself overmuch about his
son's spiritual welfare, no, but all the same he
would have been very displeased at any pranks or
escapades that might result in compromising the
family's prospects. The only person who really
appeared to take an interest in Armand-Jean's
spiritual concerns was Mgr. de Herse, the pious
Bishop of Châlons-sur-Marne. At least he was the
only one that ventured to remonstrate with the
gifted young priest who was wasting in frivolous
amusements the talents that should be employed to
advance the glory of God. Every time he met De
Rancé he would remind him of his duty as a
consecrated minister of the Gospel. '' Monsieur
l'Abbé, could you not do a little more for God
Who has given you so many lights, endowed you
with so many talents ? I am sure your own good
heart must often reproach you with the scanty
return you make to Him for all He has done for
you.'' '' If any other had done for you the
thousandth part of what the good God has done,
Monsieur, from what I know of your generous
nature, you would spend yourself unreservedly in
his service.'' As De Rancé loved the saintly old
man, he would listen respectfully to these charitable
admonitions, then would go his way rejoicing in
the thought that Paris lies at such a comfortable
distance from Châlons-sur-Marne.

But if the Bishop's words did not immediately produce the effect he desired, at least they were never forgotten. Long years afterwards when De Rancé, then regular abbot of La Trappe, was edifying the world with his austerities, it was announced to him one day that there was a man of notoriously evil life staying with the visitors in the guesthouse. " And I," he answered humbly, " what was I before my conversion ? Surrounded by the most worldly associates, and abandoned to the pleasures of the chase, I used to follow the hounds, wearing my hair long, with a sword at my side and a hunting-horn in my hand. On such occasions, and thus accoutred, I would sometimes meet a certain holy bishop who treated me with extraordinary gentleness. All he would say by way of reproof was that if only I had the goodwill I could live a little more worthily of my sacred calling." And so the poor sinner was permitted to remain in despite of the indignant brother-porter.

Now that his father was dead and his studies completed, our Abbé had more time and opportunity for indulging his passion for sport. And he did so to the full. But his priestly duties did not receive anything like the same attention. He rarely said Mass, and perhaps that was so much the better, considering how he lived. Still, he preached often, although we have reason to suspect it was rather for the glory of the Abbé de Rancé than for the glory of God. Dom Gervaise, who knew the Abbé intimately and was by no means a blind partisan of his, speaks thus of his preaching : " He was a master of that kind of eloquence which persuades, which touches, which inspires enthusiasm. His delivery was full of feeling and energy. In a word, he possessed all the qualities that go to equip the perfect orator. And these qualities he preserved to the end of his life, even under the habit of penitence. I have never met a man more capable of moving others to do what he desired of them. He had something of the same torrential eloquence which we admire in Père Bourdaloue ; but he was more affecting than the Jesuit, and spoke with more deliberation." His discourses, we are told, gained him many admirers, but made few converts. Small wonder. Does not St. Bernard say that to preach with effect, that is, with profit to souls, the whole man must preach, not the tongue alone ? And St. Paul declares that, though one should preach with the tongues of men and angels, if he has not the love of God in his heart, his words, be they never so affecting, are but as the noise of sounding brass or a tinkling cymbal.

The Abbé divided his time between Paris and Veretz : he hunted for pleasure in the capital, and for game in his baronial estate. The following description of his country residence and the incident added we have borrowed from an article contributed to the *Dublin Review*, December, 1844.

" De Rancé had a beautiful country residence at Veretz. Thither he frequently repaired when tired of the gaieties of Parisian life, or when he wished to indulge in the pleasures of the chase, of which he was excessively fond. The house at Veretz was remarkable for the magnificence of its decoration and the extent and splendour of the accommodation it afforded. Everything that wealth and taste could do—and what is there that they cannot do?—was done. The gardens and surrounding lawns were laid out with exquisite taste, and every feature of the landscape was made to harmonise with the splendour which pervaded the whole establishment. A succession of fêtes attracted from all quarters the gentry of the neighbourhood—and there were no entertainments like those of the Abbé de Rancé. When even these pleasures had palled upon the taste of their author, he determined on varying the monotony of existence by sallying forth, like some knight-errant of the olden time, in quest of adventure. It was an age of superstition too, with all its fancied refinement ; and there were many who, like Catherine de Médicis, tried to read their fate in the movements of the heavenly bodies. The tower which she built for the purpose is still, we believe, shown to the stranger in Paris. De Rancé was led by the prevailing opinions of the day ; but we should hope that there was some lingering sense of the Christian, if not of his clerical profession, and some promptings of his better nature, to save him from the folly of yielding seriously to so monstrous a delusion.

" One day at Veretz he ran great risk of losing his life. He heard in a distant part of his lawn the noise of some persons who were trespassing upon his preserves of game ; he rushed out upon them, un-armed as he was, accompanied by only a single servant, and after a short struggle disarmed the leader. But he little knew the danger to which he had exposed himself. This leader was a gentleman well known in the sporting world of that day. He was notorious for the many duels in which he had been successfully engaged—and the shedding of human blood was a thing of very little moment in his eyes. The law could not reach, and public opinion honoured, instead of stigmatising, the murderer who could show the emblems of nobility upon his escutcheon. From such an adversary and in the excitement of the chase one could scarcely hope for quarter or mercy. And after the event had taken place, the trespasser was wont to say that Providence had something yet in store for De Rancé, for though he had him in his power and feared neither God nor man, there was something, he could not tell what, that prevented him from killing the Abbé on the spot as he had intended more than once to do.''[2]

The above supplies us with an instance of the Abbé's fearless courage. Other examples will meet us on our way. The reference to knight-errantry needs a word of explanation. Our Abbé and two of his associates formed the wild project of wandering through the world in quest of adventure, each providing himself with the sum of 1,000 pistoles. Accident alone prevented the execution of their Quixotic design.

During this time of idleness and pleasure-seeking, the Abbé was rather worldly than wicked. He lived in a manner unworthy of his calling as a priest, unworthy even of his character as a Christian. There was plenty frivolity, plenty dissipation, plenty vanity and disedifying amusements. These things made up his existence. But there is no evidence that he ever went beyond them. His enemies, and God knows they were numerous and malicious enough, had to be content with suspicious and

[2] De Rancé himself gives a somewhat different account of this incident. The poachers were three in number. As soon as the Abbé accosted them the leader levelled his gun at him, but before he could pull the trigger, De Rancé wrested the weapon from his hands, then with the help of his valet disarmed the other two. At 4 o'clock in the evening, the first gentleman called at the house to apologise, and asked for the three guns. " He said I had torn the gun out of the hands of the most desperate rascal on earth, and that he thanked God he had not murdered me." On another occasion, a gentleman discharged his gun at short range and point blank at De Rancé. The pellets pierced his clothes, but inflicted no wound on his body.

gratuitous accusations. At the worst his life contained nothing of what we ordinarily mean by
scandal, no gross immorality. M. Bremond, who,
as he quite unnecessarily informs us, holds no brief
for De Rancé's character, acknowledges so much,
and certainly he would not acknowledge it were he
not convinced of its truth. It must be admitted,
however, that our Abbé loved the danger, he was
fond of disporting himself on the ice ; so that,
everything considered, the wonder is not that he
descended so low, but that he did not descend to
depths far lower. Of his relations with the Duchess
of Montbazan we shall speak further on.

CHAPTER IV.

Archdeacon—National Synod—De Rancé defends Cardinal de Retz—His Retirement from Paris—Scruples.

MEANTIME the Abbé's dissipated life must have excited some degree of public attention ; for his relatives became alarmed. It was not that they feared for his soul or lamented the dishonour done to the priesthood. Bless you, no ! They feared lest the report of his doings should come to the knowledge of the Queen, which would put an end to their hopes of seeing him honoured with the mitre. So they put their worldly-wise heads together to see what could be done. One thing was clear : the Abbé must be somehow or other got away from Paris. And here luck was on their side. It so happened that some time previous to this the archdeacon of Outre-Vienne, in the archdiocese of Tours, had died and the vacancy had not yet been filled. Just the place for the Archbishop's nephew whilst awaiting promotion to a more exalted station. It would keep him at a safe distance from the capital, and at the same time would put him on the first step of the archiepiscopal throne. The Abbé himself did not contemplate the proposal with any great degree of enthusiasm. However, he consented to the arrangement. He took up his abode in the ancestral mansion at Veretz, and from there attended to the spiritual interests of his arch-deaconry. His life went on as before, a ceaseless pursuit of worldly pleasure. Yet, strange to say, this unpriestly priest, so full of vanity and world-liness, was ever ready, even in his laxest days, to leave the hunt, or the dance, the gaming-table, or the banquet-hall for the bedside of the sick and the dying. And, stranger still, he was reputed to have a special gift for bringing such to the proper dis-positions.

An incident that occurred in the year following his appointment as archdeacon, that is, in 1655, brought out into prominence a new aspect of our Abbé's character. He gave an exhibition of moral courage which attained to the heroic ; and all the detestably mean sneers and insinuations of M. Bremond will never succeed in making it appear otherwise—to those acquainted with the facts. A General Assembly of the clergy of France was convoked to meet in Paris on October 25th. The Abbé de Rancé attended as one of the deputies of the Second Order. As might be expected, he very soon became a conspicuous figure in that clerical parliament. Of the many important questions which engaged his attention and gave scope for his eloquence we shall refer here but to one, that concerning Cardinal de Retz. It will be remembered that it was he who, as coadjutor to the Archbishop of Paris, had conferred Minor Orders, Subdiaconate and Diaconate on our Abbé. The two became fast friends. In 1651 Pope Innocent X raised De Retz to the purple. The following year Mazarin had him confined to prison on an apparently false charge of treason against the State. In 1654, whilst he was still in prison, the Archbishop of Paris having died, he, as he had the right of succession, took possession of the metropolitan see by power of attorney. Later on, he managed to escape from custody and made his way into Spain. Thence he proceeded to Rome where Innocent X received him with honour, and encouraged him to stand up for his rights. Mazarin, meanwhile, had ordered the confiscation of his temporalities and degraded the vicars-general he had appointed. From the place of his exile Cardinal de Retz addressed a letter to the General Assembly, entreating the representatives of the Church of France to espouse his cause against the tyranny of the Cardinal-Minister. The letter was read to the assembled prelates, and excited much sympathy. There seemed to be no likelihood, however, that anything would be done, for Mazarin would certainly resent their interference, and, as they knew too well, he had a summary way of dealing with his opponents.

But there was one man in that National Synod whom fear could not silence. That man bore the name of Armand-Jean le Bouthillier de Rancé. Already more than once during the sessions he had vigorously protested against the Minister's invasion of ecclesiastical rights, especially against his unjust persecution of Mgr. de Harlay, the companion of our Abbé's student-days, now Archbishop of Rouen. During the discussions of the exiled Cardinal's letter, whilst the prelates were deliberating what action, if any, should be taken, the Abbé de Rancé rose in his place to advocate the claims of justice—*fiat jus, ruat coelum*. '' I know very well,'' he concluded, '' what will be the resolution adopted by this Assembly on the question which concerns Cardinal de Retz. I know that the resolution has already been taken, and that no words of mine will avail to alter your decision. Nevertheless, I have felt it a duty to declare my sentiments. I believed I owed it to my conscience and to my honour to bear public testimony to the truth. Now I have the consolation of having defended the right and championed the cause of the Archbishop of Paris, who has been victimised in a manner condemned by the Canons and opposed to the traditions of the Church.'' Have we not here a proof of his fidelity to his father's dying injunction to put conscience and honour above all the other interests of life ?

The Abbé's speech made a deep impression. It inspired the Assembly with the courage to send a deputation to the Minister demanding the restoration of De Retz. This deputation consisted of four members : the Archbishop of Bordeaux—Henri de Béthune, another unnamed bishop, and two deputies of the Second Order, of whom one was De Rancé. The Archbishop, of course, was the spokesman. But when they came before the dreaded Minister his courage failed him—if he ever had any. Instead of making the representations he had been commissioned to make, and demanding the Primate's immediate recall, he delivered a speech full of flattery of Mazarin and his administration. Not a word about the exiled Cardinal ! De Rancé could scarcely believe his ears. Unable to dissemble his disgust and indignation at such a cowardly dereliction of duty, he there and then told Béthune very plainly what he thought of him, after which he turned to the Minister and with no mincing of words explained the mission on which the deputation had come. To the accusations made against De Retz by Mazarin he replied with spirit, refusing to be bullied by the great man. People did not often conduct themselves thus in the Minister's presence. He became angry. The Abbé de Rancé seemed to think that it was his—the mighty Mazarin's—duty to have the banner and cross borne before Cardinal de Retz. But let the Abbé beware : the Court had

E

knowledge of his activities in the Assembly : in the context the Court meant Cardinal Mazarin. To this our Abbé replied : '' If the Court has heard that I have conducted myself in the Assembly any otherwise than as becomes a man of honour and probity, the Court has been misinformed.'' No servility for Armand-Jean. The wrathful Minister determined to see to it that there should be no mitre for him either.

Cardinal de Retz was not restored. That, however, need not distress us, for although treated unjustly in the present instance, and perhaps quite as good a Christian as his persecutor, he certainly cannot be considered as a model Prince of the Church. His future career does not concern us, except at the points where it crosses De Rancé's. But before we pass on to other matters, we must here call attention to a curious phenomenon. M. Henri Bremond, who shows himself so commendably zealous for the honour of the Holy See when he has need of a stick to belabour De Rancé, is not always so particular. He tells us that ''Cardinal de Retz was disowned by Rome as a nuisance,'' by the Rome that only a short time previous had raised him to the purple ! If only he could catch his victim using such disrespectful, not to say injurious, language ! How happy, how unspeakably happy it would make him ! But coming to the historicity of the question, did the Holy See disown the Cardinal? On the contrary Pope Innocent X was unwilling to accept his resignation as Archbishop of Paris and desired him to continue in office, which De Retz did, carrying on the administration by letters from Rome. So writes the illustrious historian, M. Georges Goyau, in the *Catholic Encyclopaedia,* Article " Retz."[1]

Our Abbé's open rupture with the Cardinal-Minister must have caused something like a panic in the General Assembly. Mazarin had already given the Synod a taste of his temper. During the discussion that resulted in the deputation he kept a body of armed men posted in sight of the prelates. What violent proceedings might they not expect from him now? Rumour had it that De Rancé was to be arrested, that a *lettre de cachet* would soon send him to the Bastille or the Vincennes. Nothing of the kind happened, however. But shortly afterwards, in February, 1657, the Abbé

---

[1] In a letter to Cardinal de Retz, dated September 30th, 1654, Innocent X writes that the wonderful constancy shown by the Cardinal in his misfortunes had reflected as much honour on the Sacred College as it had suffered dishonour by his imprisonment. *Anceps quidem nobis est an vivida animi constantia, qua praeclare in adversis probata efficisti ut apostolicus senatus non minus ornamenti ex meritorum tuorum incremento acceperit quam illi videretur dignitatis ex tua captivitate detractum, etc.* For ourselves, we fail to see how this can be translated or deciphered to mean that Rome " disowned Cardinal de Retz as a nuisance." But then, of course, we are not a member of the French Academy.

finding perhaps that his influence had waned, left the Assembly and retired to Veretz.[2]

The Assembly had done him the honour to request that he would make an accurate translation of the works of St. Ephrem from the original Greek into French. He intended to undertake the task, but abandoned the project when he found that none of the available texts was free from corruptions.

What the Archbishop of Tours thought of his nephew's duel with Mazarin we can only conjecture. The mitre he had hoped to obtain for Armand-Jean seemed now further off than ever. His Grace must have been grieviously disappointed and annoyed. And, indeed, we cannot blame him. For howsoever skilful our Abbé might have been as a hunter of stags and wild boars, it cannot be denied

[2] After quitting the Assembly De Rancé went first to Commercy in Lorraine to confer with De Retz who was there in hiding, having returned to France in the too confident expectation that the General Synod would obtain his recall. Perhaps we have here the principal reason for the Abbé's retirement from Paris. M. Bremond, of course, has his own explanation. Needless to say, it does no honour to De Rancé. According to the learned Academician, the bold language of our Abbé in the Assembly and before the Minister was but stage-thunder, an effort to get into the limelight. Neither courage nor zeal for justice had any part in it : the attack was motived by vanity, the retreat by cowardice. For the withdrawal from the Assembly was the panic flight of the craven. This, no doubt, is simply ridiculous. But it constitutes a magnificent example of analysis of character. Character-analysis, as everybody knows, is the art of revealing your own character whilst you are endeavouring to diagnose your neighbour's. Hence, Mr. Sheed, the Translator of the *Abbé Tempête,* tells us he will have no difficulty in recognising M. Bremond at the General Judgment.

that as a place-hunter he was absolutely hopeless. He lacked the family gift. Honours, nevertheless, kept coming his way. During his attendance at the General Assembly he was appointed almoner to the Duke of Orleans, brother to Louis XIII. This appointment pleased him immensely, because, in spite of his worldliness and habitual dissipation, he possessed a kind and generous heart. His charity to the poor became proverbial. Nor was it only with money he helped them : he also gave them unstintedly of his time and his personal service. Many touching incidents illustrative of his generosity are recounted by his early biographers.

About this time (1657), as a result no doubt of St. Vincent de Paul's remonstrances, he began to be scrupulous with regard to the number of benefices he held. The question became a matter of discussion between himself and his friends. They maintained that although a plurality of benefices was forbidden by the canons, it was justified now by custom and dispensation. '' One need have no fear of straying from the right path,'' they argued, '' when one sees so many others walking the same way, when one travels in the company of so many learned and enlightened ecclesiastics.'' This did not satisfy the Abbé. '' It is quite true,'' he answered, '' that these dispensations are of long standing ; nevertheless it is always supposed that those who

seek them have sufficient reason for the request.
Dispensations obtained for no better reason than
insatiable cupidity do not excuse from sin. Is it not
a shame to see a single individual, often useless or
worse than useless to the Church, appropriating as
much of her property as would support several
worthy ecclesiastics? In saying this," he added
humbly, " I condemn myself, but I cannot but
speak the truth. It may be an extenuation of my
fault that the benefices I possess are not of my
own procuring. They were already in my possession
before I had light enough to understand the abuse.
But if I am guiltless in this respect, I confess I am
not without scruple for having kept them so long."
For all that, he would keep them some years longer.
We have evidence that in regard to other matters
also he had begun to realise the necessity of a
change of conduct, but lacked the courage requisite
for entering on the better course. Is not that the
disposition so well described by the pagan poet :

> " I know the good and love it too
> As what I should yet do not do " ?[1]

And by St. Paul when he wrote : " For I do not
the good which I will, but the evil which I hate,
that I do. . . . . Unhappy man that I am, who
shall deliver me from the body of this death ? The

---

[1] " Video meliora proboque, sequor pejora."

grace of God through Our Lord Jesus Christ (Rom.
vii., 15, 24, 25). Yea, only that. It was soon to
be imparted to De Rancé, but he must first be
be purified for its reception in the crucible of sharp
affliction.

CHAPTER V.

The Family of De Montbazan—De Rancé's Relations with the Duchess—Different Accounts of her Death.

THE purpose of our Abbé's relatives in sending him away from Paris was to keep him out of harm's way. But in the comparative solitude of Veretz lurked dangers as great, to say the least, as any that could be met with amidst " the madding crowds " of the capital. And this brings us to the most difficult and delicate part of our narrative, the part occupied with the account of De Rancé's relations with the Duchess de Montbazan. Most assuredly we should much prefer, and our readers we doubt not would also prefer, to let the curtain drop upon those scenes of our poor Abbé's life which have made him a joy to his cruel enemies and taxed to the uttermost the charity of his friends. That would be " a thing by far the better," if only it were possible. But it is not. The omission of reference to that unfortunate liaison would not only render this sketch incomplete, but it would make all that is to follow absolutely unintelligible. So, with whatever reluctance, we must tell once again

50

the oft-told tale. Let us say *in limine,* however, to reassure the meticulous reader, that we are about to rake up no horrors, nothing of a nature calculated to revolt him. Thank God, there was never anything of the kind. Even the keen-nosed scandalmongers who, like the poor, are always with us, have been obliged to acknowledge their failure to find evidence of anything, and, as we have said, must fain be satisfied with their surmises and their suspicions and their " likely guesses." That De Rancé, by his levity and imprudence, criminal levity and imprudence, made himself a fair target for the poisoned arrows of slander cannot be denied ; neither can it be denied that his enemies availed themselves to the full of the opportunity afforded them.

M. Denis le Bouthillier de Rancé counted amongst his most intimate friends Hercules de Rohan, Duke of Montbazan. They saw a good deal of each other both in Paris and in the country, for their rural residences were not far apart. Their families, too, became very intimate. Of M. Denis the worst that anyone could say was that he was worldly and ambitious. But worldliness and ambition were pardonable faults, almost virtues, when compared with the vices that distinguished the Duke. As a young man he had served his country loyally, and proved his valour on many a hard-fought field. Even then he could hardly be described as a model of Christian virtue. Advancing years had whitened his hair without cooling his passions, so that pro-fligacy still attended him in his old age. He was in his seventieth year when he became enamoured of Marie de Bretagne, a girl of sixteen, and demanded her hand in marriage. As wealth and title did not appear to her sufficient compensation for the serious disadvantages of the match, she peremptorily refused him. Her relatives, so it seems, took a different view of the matter. Anyhow, an appeal to the Queen-Mother, Marie de Médicis, put an end to her resistance, and so she became the Duchess of Montbazan. The old Duke had a son and daughter by a former wife living with him, either of them old enough to be the parent of the young Duchess A more unnatural situation could scarcely be conceived. It must be admitted that the Duke did not behave like a jealous husband. He gave his wife the same kind of liberty he was in the habit of taking himself. Nor did she scruple to take advantage of his insouciance. She became a society leader. Her beauty—she had the reputation of being the most beautiful woman in France—and her wit and her splendid entertainments made her house a rendezvous for the wealthy and aristocratic youth of Paris.

Of these visitors none more frequently crossed her threshold than Armand-Jean de Rancé. Nor had she for any a warmer welcome. That in itself should not surprise us, for he was a great favourite with her husband, and, besides,the most entertaining of company. Nevertheless he went oftener to her house than seemed decorous in a cleric. In 1654 the old Duke died. We are not told how many days his Duchess spent in mourning, but " when the days of her mourning were over " she resumed the pursuit of pleasure and amusement with added zest, and, of course, with greater liberty. Our Abbé's visits grew more frequent and of longer duration. Sometimes he would spend whole nights at the gaming-table in her house. He looked after her business affairs—what did she know about business ? And when both were in the country the intimacy became greater still, as the proximity of their estates rendered intercourse easy. There she would return his visits and see how he acted the host.

Such is the case against our Abbé. His enemies have made the most of it. Let us see what can be said in extenuation, if not in excuse. The Montbazans and De Rancés were family friends and neighbours, which would explain and justify a certain degree of familiarity. They were also connected by the bonds of gratitude : Gervaise tells us that Armand-Jean had rendered the Duchess some important services which would entitle him to special consideration at her hands. Then she was his senior by fifteen years, and had always, like her husband the Duke, treated him as one of her own children—of whom there were three : the reader will allow that it would not be difficult to regard the Abbé—at any age—as a child. And these children of the Duchess, the eldest only about two years junior to De Rancé—can it be supposed that they were not cognisant of the dishonour to their house, or, if cognisant, connived at it? The supposition does not commend itself. Moreover, the slightest approach to impropriety was never once observed between the two, notwithstanding the sharpness of the jealous eyes that kept them under surveillance. Finally, in the library of Angers has been lately discovered a note, supposed to have been written by Arnauld, Bishop of that city during the life-time of De Rancé, which affirms that " the Abbot of La Trappe never loved the Duchess otherwise than as a friend."[2] But whatever may be thought of this, the mutual attachment was undoubtedly strong and tender.

On the 26th of April, 1657, the news reached De Rancé, then in Paris, that the Duchess de Montbazan lay dangerously ill in one of her town houses. He went at once to her bedside, and saw to his grief that the report did not exaggerate. She was dying, succumbing to an attack of measles. And no one in the household had the courage to warn her of her condition, so that she would have an opportunity to make her peace with God. Would the Abbé be so kind as to perform this office of

[2] Cf. *L'Abbé de Rancé et Bossuet,* p. 46.

charity? Yes, he would; although it was doubtless the most painful task he had ever undertaken. " There seems to be no hope," he said to her, " that you will recover from your present illness. Therefore, whilst you have still the time make haste to reconcile yourself with your Judge." She received the announcement with unexpected calmness. So she must die soon? Very well. She would immediately attend to the business of preparing. In order to free herself from all distraction, she gave the Abbé charge of her temporal affairs. Then, sending for her parish priest, she put her spiritual affairs in order. De Rancé was constantly in and out of the sick-room. On April 28th, the third day of her illness, mounting the stairs to visit her, he met her son, the Prince de Soubise, who informed him that she had just expired. She died in the forty-fifth year of her age.

The above is the generally accepted account of the sad end of a wasted life. We have neither time nor space to discuss M. Bremond's " likely guesses," desperate endeavours to prove that it was not for nothing he was made a member of the Academy. Of course, all the other biographers are wrong; for otherwise his guesses would be wrong— *quod absit*. It reminds us of the trooper who complained that the whole regiment was out of step with him.

Another and very different account of the

Duchess's end came into circulation some time after the sad event, we know not from what source. It is a gruesome narrative, demonstrably false in one part at least, highly improbable as a whole, unsubstantiated by the testimony of a single known witness, and rejected by all biographers, with the exception of Chateaubriand and, of course, Bremond who thinks there may be something in it. He is not in the least influenced by the fact that De Rancé, interrogated on the point in his old age by the Duke de Saint-Simon, unequivocally pronounced the narrative a fable. But as he wants the ugly tale we shall make him a present of it. It does not tell for or against De Rancé. The fable runs as follows :

The Abbé was staying at Veretz when he got word that the Duchess lay grievously ill in Paris. Making all haste to the capital, he arrived at her residence, and hurried at once to her room. The servants did not dare inform him of what had occurred : perhaps they did not get time. On entering the chamber, the first object that met his horrified gaze was a coffin, and near it he noticed a severed head all streaming with blood. He recognised it as the head of the Duchess. The undertaker, so it appeared, finding that the coffin was made too short for the body, adopted the horrible expedient of decapitating the corpse to avoid the labour and expense of another coffin.

Such is this precious story in its main outlines, for it has varied much with regard to the trimmings in the hands of different writers. Chateaubriand gives it, as might be expected, with a wealth of picturesque detail which less imaginative romancers could not hope to emulate.

The Abbé had been aware from his first visit to the sick-room that he must very soon lose the Duchess Marie, whatever she may have been to him. But he did not realise fully what her loss would mean. The excitements of these past days, his compassion for her sufferings, and above all his anxious solicitude for the welfare of her soul, allowed him no time for reflection. Hence, he was quite unprepared for the announcement of her death. The shock nearly killed him. He fainted on the staircase, and had to be helped to his house. There he was visited by the priest who had attended the dying woman ; the assurance given him by the good curé that she had expired in the most edifying dispositions brought some consolation to his broken heart.

CHAPTER VI.

*Desolation and Conversion—Mother Louise—Père
    Seguenot—De Rancé Goes to Paris—Disap-
    pointments.*

DE RANCÉ, it appears, did not wait for the funeral.
He could no longer endure the Paris which had
heretofore been his heaven on earth, indeed the
only heaven he bothered his head about. Everything there reminded him of her whose tragic taking
off left his heart and the whole world empty. So
the very day of her death saw him posting to his
country house at Veretz. But if he hoped thereby
to escape from his grief he was sadly disappointed.
"Veretz," writes the eloquent Chateaubriand,
paraphrasing the prosaic account of Gervaise,
"which was once so agreeable a residence, now
became insupportable to De Rancé. Its magnificence was revolting to him : the furniture, which
everywhere sparkled with silver and gold ; the
gorgeous beds where even luxury—to use the words
of a standard writer of the times—would have found
itself too comfortable ; the rooms, hung with
pictures of great price ; the gardens, so exquisitely
laid out : all this was too much for a man who now

looked at everything through a shower of falling tears."

The image of the dead Duchess haunted him : he beheld it whithersoever he turned. And his tortured mind kept ceaselessly asking the unanswerable question : where is she now ? Aye, there was the rub. If she were lost could he disclaim responsibility ? He was a priest, he had had great influence over her, and nevertheless he had allowed her, without a word of warning, to travel along that broad and pleasant way that leads to perdition, yea, and even encouraged her by his example. " He wished to bury himself in the shade of his forest trees, and to recover his peace of mind in silence and alone. He took long walks in the woods and fields about him, to try to get rid of the weight that was pressing upon his heart. He wandered about in his gardens amid sweet-smelling flowers, and shrubs fragrant with the odours of far-off lands, hoping that his mind would be diverted thereby from the horrible thought that was pressing upon his brain, and goading him well-nigh to madness. He wandered by running streams on the surrounding hills, and watched their crystal waters as they ran in murmuring whispers along their pebbly bed, and wished to forget the world and the world's cares ; but there was a harrowing remembrance that followed him even there. He reclined upon the greensward, or sat in some shady arbour of his own princely

domain, or gazed upon the many forms of sculp-
tured beauty which for years had been collected
within its walls, and asked himself why he should
not be happy and at ease? But a spirit was evoked
which would not suffer him to be at rest; and
whithersoever he turned himself, to what distraction
soever he gave himself—whether in his hours of
forced occupation in the sullen loneliness and silence
of his chamber, whether in the world's noise or the
midnight darkness or the glare of noon—that
countenance, so sad, so horrible, cast its reproach-
ful look upon him.''

It has been said that he applied to the occult
sciences of astrology and necromancy in the wild
hope of obtaining an answer to the terrible doubt
that tormented him; he is also said to have seen
the Duchess in vision floating in a pool of fire and
giving utterance to heart-rending shrieks. The latter
story Gervaise—who knew as much about De
Rancé's career as anybody—puts aside as a piece
of fiction. We may probably treat in the same way
the story of his having recourse to the Black Art.

De Rancé's dream of earthly happiness had come
to an end; the mirage had suddenly vanished,
leaving that world, which had hitherto appeared so
beautiful to his eyes, as unhomelike as a howling
wilderness. His heart was riven, but not yet converted. The danger now was one of utter despair and
complete infidelity. Suffering and disillusionment do

not always bring the sinner to God, nor do humiliations always make him humble. In this case,
however, grace proved triumphant. Perhaps the
Abbé owed that victorious grace to the prayers of
the grateful poor to whom he had ever shown himself
so generous. Perhaps his pious mother to whose
counsels he had paid so little heed, and the many
souls he had assisted in their agony, redoubled their
intercession for him in that his hour of need, the hour
which was to decide whether he would become a fol-
lower of the great Augustine or a forerunner of De
Lamenais. However that may have been, he came
forth from the fiery ordeal a new man, with a new
philosophy of life and new ambitions. He now saw
clearly by the light of a revived faith that there was
a beneficent purpose in the calamities which had
overtaken him. The thunderbolts of heaven had
shattered his idols because God desired to draw
him even thus to Himself. He understood at the
same time that God and God only could fill the
void He had made in his poor heart. " I had never
ceased to believe in Him," he wrote long afterwards, referring to his conversion, " and I did not
doubt that I should find Him in my great need.
Yea, I entertained the hope that He would Himself
fill the immense void He had made in my heart by
emptying it of the love of creatures." So peace
returned to his spirit after more than three months
of storm.

He began to apply himself to meditation and spiritual reading. " I had to do violence to myself in order to read books for which I had never any taste. I recalled to mind the different virtues, whereof it could be said that I knew nothing of them so far beyond the name. However, I tried to practise them. I recognised their importance, and I felt convinced that only in the practice of them with a lively faith was any real happiness to be found." The sentiments that appeared uppermost in his mind at the beginning of his conversion were those of contrition for the past, humility at the view of his utter wretchedness, an ardent desire of penance, and deep gratitude to God Who had saved him from such danger and almost in spite of himself. They were to become the virtues that would dominate his soul and give colour and shape to his spirituality. In order to preserve and foster his sense of gratitude, he at this time made a list of the many occasions whereon Divine Providence had delivered him from " a sudden and unprovided death." There are thirteen instances enumerated. At the end of the list we find the words : *Et de his omnibus eripuit me Dominus*. As he pondered over the dangers to which he had been exposed, he would exclaim : " O my poor Abbé de Rancé, if you had died then, where would you now be ?"

" Lord, what wilt Thou have me to do ?" cried the humbled Saul, stricken down on the road to

Damascus. And he was sent for instruction to
Ananias. An Ananias must be found for our Abbé
too, but where? "Forasmuch as those persons of my
acquaintance in the world," so he wrote at a later
period to one of his penitents, Madame de la
Fayette, " who made profession of piety did not
commend themselves to me, which, as I knew, was
not their fault but rather mine, I saw no one to
whom I could give my confidence. Thus, finding
myself as a stranger in an unknown land, I spent
several months in perplexity and agitation, not knowing very well what course I ought to take." The
reader will please observe that our Abbé does not
say he could find no pious person qualified to act
as his director, but that the persons of that description whom he knew were not to his liking[3]—quite
a different matter. Yet M. Bremond has this
comment on the above-quoted passage: " Not, be
it noted, that there was any dearth of saints at the
time, but Rancé could never manage to find any,
save in history. They seemed to have gone on
strike after St. Bernard." It is a good illustration
of the Academician's sharp practice.

During the period of his hopeless grief and for
several months after his conversion, De Rancé
lived the life of a hermit at Veretz. He had fully

---

[3] *Comme les personnes que j'avais vues dans le monde et
qui faisaient profession de piété ne me revenaient pas, je
crus que ce n'etait pas leur faute, mais la mienne, je n'en
voyais point á qui je puisse donner ma confiance.*

made up his mind to give himself henceforth entirely and irrevocably to the service of God, but wished to know what service was required of him. In his doubt he bethought him of a holy nun living in the convent of the Visitation which his uncle, the Archbishop, had established at Tours. This religious Mother Louise, had been only too well known in the world by the name Louise Testu le Roger de la Mardeliere, the favourite mistress of Duke Gaston of Orleans. Now, however, she was as distinguished for her virtues as she had formerly been for her vices. Our Abbé decided to consult her about his vocation. She referred him to Père Seguenot, an Oratorian, once an eminent advocate, who, like De Rancé himself, had experienced the bitterness of disillusionment and owed his conversion to the blighting of his worldly hopes.

To this disciple of St. Philip he opened his mind. He told him of his resolutions and aspirations, and requested to know what God required of him. He would resign all his benefices except one, make restitution for the ecclesiastical property employed in profane uses by himself and his father, and live thenceforth in retirement, aloof from the distractions and dangers of the world. Furthermore, he desired to sell all his possessions immediately and distribute the proceeds to the poor. " For me," he argued, " this is not a mere counsel : it is a precept." The good Oratorian was overjoyed to discover such dispositions in his penitent, but being a man of prudence, he counselled him to put his resolutions to the test of time. The sacramental absolution also he judged it wise to defer : Père Seguenot belonged to the rigorist school of moralists. Finally he recommended the Abbé to take counsel with certain of his brother Oratorians in Paris who, he said humbly, were better qualified to direct him than he was himself. De Rancé felt deeply disappointed at the decision to postpone absolution, as he was eager to resume the celebration of Holy Mass. But he submitted without a word.

Acting on the confessor's advice he hastened to Paris. His reappearance in the capital after so long an absence must have caused quite a sensation. He had, of course, been already made the subject of much gossip. The mystery of his relations with the late Duchess de Montbazan, and the manner in which her tragic death had affected the Abbé, stimulated the public imagination to an unusual degree. The professionally pious were given a chance to practise a little hypocrisy, and others who made no pretensions to piety got a golden opportunity for the exercise of their wit. For the Pharisees and the humorists De Rancé felt the same indifference. But there was another class of Parisians that inspired him with fear. Certain high-born ladies came to express their sympathy for the loss he had sustained and offered to take the place of the deceased Duchess in his regard. They were promptly shown the door.

This adventure warned him that he must not delay longer in Paris than was absolutely necessary. So he went at once to the Oratory and asked for Father Bouchard. This priest had a history somewhat resembling his own; he had sown his wild oats with a liberal hand, and turned sincerely to God after a youth of dissipation. The population of seventeenth-century France included a large percentage of returned Prodigals and reconciled Magdalens. To Père Bouchard our Abbé made a general confession, and this time, so it seems, was given absolution. He met another member of the same community who impressed him even more favourably than did the good religious to whom he had confessed. This was Father de Mouchy, who at that time enjoyed an extraordinary reputation as a director of souls. Not less was his reputation for personal holiness, whilst his humility made him refuse all ecclesiastical preferments. Once on being told there was question of making him a bishop, he replied: " I am neither saint enough nor sinner enough for such an office." He advised the Abbé to place at the disposal of God in some one of the Active Orders his erudition and the rare talents with which he was endowed. Several other enlightened directors gave him the same counsel. But he felt an unshakeable conviction that he was called to something quite different. What about the foreign missions in India or Canada? said others. There you would have all the privations and austerities you desire. Nay, you would even have hopes of attaining the crown of martyrdom. The prospect pleased him. " How happy I should be, O Lord," he cried, " to give my blood and my life for Thee."

But, like St. Philip Neri, he heard, or thought he heard, an interior voice assuring him that a mission and a martyrdom awaited him indeed, but neither amid the Indian jungles nor the Canadian snows. His counsellors must have thought him hard to please; perhaps they even doubted the sincerity of his professions. " Thou knowest, O Lord," he exclaimed in anguish, " Thou knowest the desires of my heart, and that I seek nothing save Thyself alone. Show me, I entreat, the way by which Thou wouldst have me come to Thee." Does it not recall the solemn protestation which the distressed Apostle made at daybreak on the lake-shore when *his* sincerity also seemed called in question: " Lord, Thou knowest all things, Thou knowest that I love Thee "? So the Abbé was obliged to return to Veretz with his doubts unresolved. God would make known His Will unmistakably but in His own good time. Meantime there was nothing for it but to wait in patience.

Now this was a thing De Rancé found exceedingly

difficult to do. Delays of any kind made him fretful and fidgety. He loved swiftness in everything : his biographers inform us that when in the world he always travelled at top speed, and that so little patience had he that he wanted to see the end of every enterprise almost before he had made a beginning. We know from his letters how he fretted at the length of time he was obliged to wait before each of his university examinations. And his last words will be an expression of holy impatience indeed, but still impatience : *Deus meus ne tarda-veris*. He needed consequently the discipline of his present check.

CHAPTER VII.

Life of Retreat at Veretz—A Project prevented by
the Death of the Duke of Orleans—Bishops
Pavillon, du Plessis-Praslin and de Caulet—
Thoughts of La Grande Chartreuse—De Rancé
disposes of his Property.

THE time of waiting, however, did not pass without
profit. Two priests came to Veretz to share his
penance and his solitude. They drew up a horarium
fixing the hours for Mass, Divine Office, mental
prayer, spiritual reading, manual labour, meals,
time of retiring and rising. Their food was coarse
and scanty, the time for sleeping short. The Abbé
would have given all he possessed to the poor did
not his confessor restrain him. This penitential
life at Veretz can be compared with the retreat of
St. Augustine and his companions at Cassiacum,
with the sojourn of St. Bernard and his relatives at
Chatillon, and with the retirement of the Tractarians
under Newman at Littlemore. That De Rancé
suffered much during this period of preparation may
be gathered from a remark he made at the time,
and which has been preserved by Gervaise : " How
strange is the life of a Christian ! One must keep

the pruning-knife always in one's hand, and the incisions must be made to reach even the most intimate affections of the heart. And there is no rest for us in this world until we put ourselves in the place where God would have us be.'' Yet, to a correspondent who compassionated him for his lonely life, he wrote : '' I assure you, Monsieur, I am staying in this place only on account of the happiness I find here. And my books, with what little reflection I am capable of, afford me so much and such constant contentment that I should be a fool to quit this sweet and peaceful abode for another where I know from experience neither peace nor happiness is to be found.'' Of the incidents of the years 1658—1659 connecting him with M. Arnauld d'Andilly and Port-Royal we shall speak further on when we come to discuss his attitude towards Jansenism.

His worldly friends imagined at first that this retirement was due to a passing fit of fervour, like that which led him to the Chartreuse after his ordination, and so they left him in peace. But as soon as they perceived that he intended to abandon the world in earnest and for good, they began to devise means to drag him forth from his shelter. His uncle, the Archbishop, showed himself particularly insistent. He reminded his nephew of the terrible account he would have to render to God for talents unemployed and for souls lost, and told him also of the railleries of which he was the object, and which tended to the dishonour of his family. The good man only wasted his words. Our Abbé's resolution was not to be shaken.

During the spring and summer of 1659 he made a visitation of the various religious establishments of which he was commendatory superior. It was the first time he had ever discharged this duty. The condition in which he found some of the communities did not contribute very much to his comfort and peace of mind.

Towards the end of the same year, the light he had been waiting for appeared to have come at last. Gaston, brother to Louis XIII and Duke of Orleans, who, like himself had reformed his life and was now living as a decent Christian in his palace at Blois, communicated to him his design of retiring into the forest of Chambord, and there devoting himself exclusively to the care of his soul. Perhaps the Abbé would like to accompany him? The Abbé would be only too delighted. He saw in the proposal a manifestation of God's Will. Besides, the Grandmontine priory of Boulogne which he held *in commendam* lay right in the densest part of the forest, and sheltered only a few religious. All was arranged. The Duke intended to bring nine more companions, all inspired with the same purpose as animated himself.

Our Abbé returned to Veretz with a light heart.

He came this time not to stay but put his affairs in order. All his valuable furniture, not yet disposed of, must be sold for the benefit of the poor. As he passed from apartment to apartment of that magnificent house and recalled the words of the Gospel : " Wo to you that are rich," " Wo to you that now laugh," " It is easier for a camel to pass through the eye of a needle than for a rich man to enter into the kingdom of God," he exclaimed in terror : " O my God, where am I ? Either the Gospel deceives us or this house is the home of a reprobate."

An incident that occurred at this time made a deep impression on his mind. " One day," he writes, " I met a poor shepherd, about sixty years of age, who, whilst tending his flock in the fields, had been obliged to seek shelter from a shower under a tree. As he appeared to me a man of extraordinarily cheerful aspect, I asked him if he found pleasure in his daily occupation. He replied that his work gave him perfect contentment, that it was a delight to him to look after these simple and innocent creatures, that his days seemed no longer than moments, that he enjoyed so much happiness in his humble condition that he would not exchange it for anything in the world, in fine that he would not wish to leave this earth for heaven if he thought there would be no fields above and no flocks to tend there. I admired this

good man's simplicity. And comparing him with
the world's great ones whose ambition is never
satisfied, who never say *satis* even when they have
acquired all the wealth and honours and pleasures
which this life can afford, I began to see that it
is not in the possession of earthly goods our
happiness consists, but rather in purity of morals,
in simplicity and moderation of desires, in the re-
trenchment of all things not absolutely indispensable,
in submission to the Will of God, in the love and
esteem of the state wherein He has placed us.''

Towards the end of January, 1660, a messenger
arrived at Veretz from Blois with the news that
the Duke lay dangerously ill. The Abbé hastened
to the bedside of his friend, and remained with him
until February 2nd, feast of the Purification, when
that Prince redeemed a worthless and wayward life
by a truly Christian death. A holy death after a
life of sin—God be praised for His unspeakable
mercies ! De Rancé felt wonderfully consoled.
But the hope, so fondly fostered, of a prayerful
retreat in the forest of Chambord—that had died
with Duke Gaston.

Back to Veretz again. Would he never behold
the heavenly beacon that should light his way
through the swirling waters to the haven of peace ?
Nevertheless, he was determined to make no move
until he had a clear intimation as to God's holy
Will. On this subject he wrote to his friend, Mother

Louise : " We ought never to leave the position in which God has placed us until He Himself withdraws us therefrom. He alone has the right to make us quit the post He has assigned us. . . . . You know that it is only necessary to be a Christian in order to be convinced of the obligation to make God the end of even our least actions. How much more so when there is question of the most important actions of our life ?"

The Abbé now turned for counsel to the friend of his youth, the pious Bishop of Châlons-sur-Marne. Not being able himself to give him definite guidance, or rather unwilling like so many others to undertake that responsibility, this worthy prelate referred him to Mgr. Pavillon, Bishop of Aleth. Had any one inquired at that time : who was the holiest Bishop in France ? the answer he would receive from every well-informed person would undoubtedly be : Monseigneur Pavillon. His reputation for eminent sanctity seemed as well established and as well deserved as was that of St. Francis de Sales half a century before. He had been the favourite disciple of St. Vincent de Paul, who used to call him his " right arm." Being nominated bishop, nothing could induce him to accept the proferred dignity until St. Vincent said to him : " If you persist in your refusal, I myself shall rise up against you at the judgment-seat of God, together with all the souls that will have perished in the diocese as the result of your obstinate disobedience.'' That, of course, rendered further resistance impossible. Pavillon went to Aleth amid the Pyrenees where he began to discharge his episcopal duties in a way worthy of the apostolic age. Such was the man recommended to our Abbé as the person best qualified to enlighten him with regard to his vocation. He wrote to the Bishop, explaining everything that he judged necessary or helpful to guide him to a decision, and begged to be shown the way wherein he should walk. For answer he was told that a question of such importance could not be settled by correspondence but by conference : if the Abbé de Rancé would find it convenient to make a journey to Aleth, Monseigneur Pavillon would be happy to talk things over with him. But Aleth was so far distant and so difficult of access !

The Bishop's letter disappointed our Abbé. These endless conferences that resulted in leaving him as perplexed as he was before ! He was sick and tired of them. He would now strike out for himself, and flee without further delay to the silence and solitude of La Grande Chartreuse, there to pass the remainder of his life amongst the austere sons of St. Bruno. His friend and former tutor, the Abbé Favier, engaged to accompany him. Not, so it appears, that he intended to don the religious habit —he had still '' a horrible aversion '' for the monastic dress—but to live in the monastery as a permanent boarder, or perhaps as an oblate, applying himself exclusively to the concerns of his soul. The Archbishop of Tours, hearing of what was afoot, took the alarm and sent for his nephew. A letter written by the latter gives us an account of the interview. " His Grace of Tours and myself discussed my affairs with not a little temper. However, my resolution stood firm. I will carry it out in spite of the whole world. . . . . He offered me an important charge in the archdiocese, that is, the direction of all the communities of nuns. You may be sure I felt little inclined to accept that. My reasons for refusing were these : first, I don't think the charge is one that should be given to young priests ; second, I consider one ought to have learned to direct oneself before undertaking the direction of others."

Before he could put his design into execution something occurred that once more put doubts into his mind as to whether, after all, he was called to live with the Carthusians. Mgr. du Plessis-Praslin, Bishop of Saint Bertrand-de-Comminges, returning to his diocese from Paris, visited Veretz, and persuaded De Rancé to accompany him home : there he would find himself not far from Aleth where Mgr. Pavillon was expecting him. Our Abbé seems to have enjoyed the journey which he made in the Bishop's coach. In Du Plessis-Praslin he was edified to perceive " those qualities so rarely to be seen in persons of his profession : capacity, charity, gentleness, cordiality, vigilance." Still more edified was he on arriving at Aleth. The episcopal palace excited his wonder and at once called up the image of his own house at Veretz. Never had he seen a poorer dwelling than this " palace." Of hangings or even furniture he could observe none, except a couple of camp-stools in the miserable cell which Mgr. Pavillon occupied. For himself, he was provided with a good dinner, but he noticed that the Bishop contented himself with a few almonds. " I have at last come to Aleth," he writes enthusiastically, " and I find that the sanctity of the Bishop exceeds all my anticipations ; I doubt if anything comparable to it can be found upon the earth. This also I can say, that only in a few persons have I beheld such enlightenment combined with such humility. His austerity is indeed very great. Nevertheless, with regard to himself and others he acts in accordance with those rules of conduct laid down by Truth Itself, to none better known than to him. His kindness could not be surpassed. I should have been more surprised at his extreme goodness to myself, did I not know that he treats everybody in just the same way, even his enemies, those—namely, whom his duty obliges him to rebuke . . . . His doctrine is sound and orthodox : no errors whether of theory or of practice have found access to this place."

" Sell your share of the paternal inheritance, repair the damaged churches with the revenues from your various benefices, and give what remains to the Hôtel-Dieu or the Hôpital Général." This time the Abbé had no cause to complain of want of definiteness or of strictness in the counsel tendered. It took his breath away. " But, Monseigneur, I shall thus be sure to arouse the anger of my family." " My dear sir, I thought you desired to know from me, not what would best please your relatives, but what you ought to do so as to discharge your conscience. Has not Christ declared : ' He that loveth father or mother more than Me is not worthy of Me' ?" He was bound, moreover, to learn and fulfil all the duties of a commendatory abbot.

But Mgr. Pavillon would not approve of the Abbé's retiring to La Grande Chartreuse : he should rather seek his own sanctification in contributing actively to the salvation and sanctification of others. One morning, at daybreak, he invited his visitor to accompany him on his pastoral rounds. They travelled all day on foot over mountains and moors, through fields and forests, accosting every soul they met, entering the cabins of the poor, joining the labourers at their work ; and the Bishop had a message for each : consolation for some, encouragement for others, reproof for these, entreaty for those, instruction and charity for all. On their return, he said to the Abbé : "Don't you think this kind of life would be as penitential as that which you propose to lead in the desert ? Remain yet a while in retreat, as did St. Augustine, in order to purify yourself from the world's contagion. But your vocation, like that of every priest, is to serve the Church by ministering to souls. *Ite, docete omnes gentes.*"

The sojourn at Aleth lasted six weeks. From there our Abbé went to see Mgr. de Caulet, Bishop of Pamiers, another of the disciples of St. Vincent de Paul. His advice regarding the revenues agreed with Pavillon's, but he further recommended his visitor to live retired in one of the religious houses which he held *in commendam*. Here was something new. On his way home, he called again on Mgr. du Plessis-Praslin, to tell him the result of his consultations. "My advice to you," said that holy Bishop, "is this : become a monk in earnest." "What ! I become a monk ! Preposterous !" The word of the Lord had come to him at last. But he had little welcome for it. In all his dreams and projects of immolating himself for God, this idea, strange to say, had never occurred to him. And now when it was presented to his mind, he put it away with something like horror.

No sooner had he arrived home than he began to reduce to practice the counsels given him at Aleth and Pamiers. His relatives, as he anticipated, were all up in arms the moment they learned of his purpose to dispose of his possessions. But he paid no attention to their remonstrances and complaints. He refused an offer for Veretz from his brother-in-law, Count d'Albon, and sold it at a higher price to a stranger, because he would not betray the interests of the poor, for whom the proceeds were intended. Of his benefices, he handed over the richest—Notre Dame-du-Val—to the Carthusians; but as the King, Louis XIV, under the influence of the same Count d'Albon, refused his consent to the transfer, that benefice passed ultimately into private but worthy hands. Saint-Symphorien de Beauvais went to his old and faithful friend, the Abbé Favier. To the Hôtel-Dieu he presented his two town houses. His servants were all amply indemnified for the loss of their positions. And when he had satisfied all other claims and charges, he had still on hand one hundred thousand crowns to be distributed amongst the poor. He still retained two of his benefices, La Trappe and the Grandmontine priory of Boulogne. The reason was that, being determined to follow the advice of the Bishop of Pamiers, he intended to retire into one or other of these houses, but remained still undecided as to which he ought to choose. His personal taste inclined him strongly in favour of Boulogne, with its encompassing girdle of forest trees. The associations of Chambord too attracted him thither. But he no longer regulated his conduct by the rules of inclination or taste.

He had thus fulfilled one part of the counsel of perfection : he had sold what he possessed and given the price to the poor.[2] It only remained for him now to follow the Master. That also he was determined to do, to follow Him without ever once looking back, to follow Him even to the summit of Calvary, to the exaltation of the Cross. Only he did not yet know clearly where his Calvary, where his crucifixion was to be. So at the end of July, 1662, in the thirty-sixth year of his age, he left Veretz for ever, that beautiful home where he had tasted the extremes of joy and sorrow, and directed his course for La Trappe. He wished merely to inspect the monastery, to see how it would answer his purpose as a place of retreat and life-long seclusion from the world. Most certainly he had no thought of taking the religious habit there.

[2] He still retained a considerable sum destined to defray the expenses of much-needed repairs in the monasteries of La Trappe and Boulogne; but this money also may be regarded as given to the poor. His library, which was very valuable, he donated to La Trappe.

CHAPTER VIII.

La Trappe—Its Occupants—Monsieur de Saint-
Louis—La Trappe occupied by Cistercians of
the Strict Observance—De Rancé's Relations
with the Monks—He decides to take the Habit—
Interview with Dom Jouaud—Conversions.

THE monastery known as Our Lady of La Trappe
occupies a secluded valley in the diocese of Seez,
in the modern Department of Orne, about eighty-
four miles south-west from Paris. It already had
a long and chequered history before it became
associated with the name of Armand-Jean de
Rancé. Its existence began in the year of grace
1122, when Rotrou II, Count of Perche, built a
votive chapel on a part of his domain called La
Trappe, a term which, in the patois of the locality,
signified the Steps : a flight of steps led down to
the ponds or lakes where the people were accustomed to fish. The chapel stood in the midst of
these lakes, and was so constructed as to present
the appearance of a ship inverted ; for it commem-
orated the Count's deliverance from shipwreck in
1120, and the sinking of the *Blanche-Nef* in the
English Channel the same year, with the loss of

all on board, including his fiancée, Matilda, daughter of Henry I of England, her brothers William, Crown Prince, and Richard, and about three hundred of the nobility. Later on the Count built there a large church, of the same shape as the original chapel, and a monastery which he gave to the Congregation of Savigny, a branch of the Benedictine Order. When this Congregation became affiliated to the Order of Citeaux in 1147, the Cistercian Observance was introduced into La Trappe.

The abbey prospered wonderfully in its new allegiance. For more than two hundred years it maintained its reputation as a nursery of saints. The wars which devastated Normandy at the close of the fourteenth century did not spare that asylum of peace : the monks were obliged to abandon the monastery, but only for awhile. In 1527 appeared a worse enemy than the wild warriors of the earlier period. The monastery in that year became the prey of a commendatory abbot, and continued to be held *in commendam* until 1662. This substitution of a commendatory for a regular abbot was attended with the usual—we might almost say inevitable results. Discipline relaxed, the community dwindled, even its material prosperity began rapidly to decline. When De Rancé arrived at the place in 1662, he found the monastery looking like an abandoned ruin. It was inhabited by half a dozen persons who called themselves monks, but did not deserve to be called Christians. They did not even make pretence of observing any rule and they lived by their wits. The Abbé's heart sank at sight of them. So these were his spiritual children! God help him! Yet such as they were, he had serious responsibilities with regard to them, and their present lamentable condition was due, in part at least, to his neglect of such responsibilities. Was it yet too late? Could anything be done to restore discipline and fervour in this unsightly ruin which had been erected unto the glory of God? He would try, at all events.

He set himself to soften the hearts of these barbarians and to inspire them with the fear and love of God. All his powers of persuasion were enlisted in the undertaking. According to St. Paul's recommendation, he preached the word, he was instant in season and out of season, he reproved, entreated, rebuked in all patience and doctrine. The patience and gentleness he displayed would have melted hearts less hard than iron, but made no impression on these, except to exasperate them. His charitable endeavours were met with insult and outrage. Nevertheless he persisted, always mindful of God's long-suffering mercy towards himself. But at last, when he could not any longer shut his eyes to the futility of his efforts, he called the six together and told them plainly his determination to

restore La Trappe to its original purpose, to make
it again a house of prayer and penance according to
Cistercian rule : if they or any of them were willing
to assist him to attain that object, their co-operation
would be welcomed, but if they attempted to oppose
him he would make them repent of it. This address
was received with uproar. What ! Introduce
reform ? Subject them to discipline ? Impose
restraints on their liberty and silence on their
tongues ? Never ! Let him just try it and he would
see ! They were not going to change their manner
of life at the bidding of this arrogant intermeddler,
this *blasé* libertine.

The clamour grew so loud that a gentleman
listening outside became alarmed for the Abbé's
safety, and hurried to call assistance. M. de Saint-
Louis, a distinguished military officer living at some
leagues' distance was quickly on the spot. The
Abbé thanked him, but declared he had no need of
assistance. " He reminded me," writes the officer,
" that the affairs of God must not be conducted in
the same manner as worldly affairs "—De Saint-
Louis evidently wanted to try the temper of his
blade on the malcontents—" that there is little use
in forcing men to do what is good unless you teach
them to love the good. During our conversation I
observed in him an air of extraordinary grandeur,
and a most exquisite politeness. Above all, he
showed such a tranquillity of mind as if he were

absolutely indifferent to the danger that threatened him. And it was quite evident that he had a very real affection for those miserable wretches.''

Finding appeals to their conscience unavailing, the Abbé threatened to report the recalcitrants to the King. This had the desired effect. They promised submission and the reform of their conduct. Without giving them time to change their mood, he sent for the Abbot of Barbery, an abbey belonging to the Cistercians of the Strict Observance, situated in the diocese of Bayeux. On the arrival of this prelate, De Rancé assembled his flock, we had almost said his pack, and made a final appeal to them. In conclusion he said that those who wished to remain and to live the Citsercian life would receive every encouragement, the others were free to depart with a liberal retiring pension. Three elected to remain, one of them, at least, destined to die in the odour of sanctity. An arrangement was then made with the Abbot of Barbery whereby La Trappe became the possession of the monks of the Strict Observance.

Immediately a colony of monks came from the monastery of Perseigne, in the diocese of Mans, Department of Sarthe, to take possession. The state in which they beheld the once glorious abbey of Our Lady of La Trappe brought tears to their eyes. But to them it might be said as once to the Israelites who lamented the vanished glory of the

first temple : " Yet now take courage, all ye
people of the land, for thus saith the Lord of
Hosts : Yet a little while and I will move the
heaven and the earth, and the sea and the dry
land, and I will fill this house with glory, saith the
Lord of Hosts . . . . Great shall be the glory of
this last house more than of the first ; and in this
place I will give peace, saith the Lord of Hosts "
(Aggeus ii., 5-10).

The difficulty of restoring these tottering ruins
to the condition of a habitable monastery seemed to
the new arrivals so great that De Rancé had all he
could do to prevent them from giving up in despair.
He was himself full of courage and of confidence in
the divine assistance. To give them heart, he made
over to them the estate set aside for the support of
the abbot—the mensal lands[1]—and promised to
provide the means of defraying a great part of the
expense that should be incurred. They laboured

---

1 Partly as the cause but chiefly as the effect of the
commendatory system, the monastic property was divided into
two parts. One part, called the *mense abbatiale,* was appro-
priated exclusively to the abbot's use, so that he might be
able to maintain his status. The other part, *mense con-
ventuelle,* belonged to the community : they were expected to
support themselves on its revenues, and also to keep the
monastery in good repair. The abbot had also his private
residence—the abbatial manse—where he stayed when visiting the abbey, and where he entertained his friends. We
have said that this arrangement was, to some extent, the
cause of the commendatory system, because it was just this
separation of revenues, already existing, that in many cases
made the abbatial dignity seem desirable to worldly persons
either as an object of ambition or as a suitable means of
rewarding services rendered. *Hinc lacrymae rerum.*

with such zeal and diligence that by the 20th of August (St. Bernard's feast day) of the same year, 1662, the work of restoration was sufficiently advanced to permit the practice of regular community life. That auspicious day witnessed in La Trappe the resumption of monastic observance, after so long an interruption. Once more the Divine Office was chanted in the church at the appointed times, silence and recollection came back to the cloisters, and the various exercises succeeded each other according to the usual horarium.

The Abbé took part in all the labours and austerities of the monks. He shared their fasts and abstinence, their silence and recollection too so far as his duties permitted, and attended their Offices in choir. By this time he had fully satisfied himself that it was God's Will he should make La Trappe his home. So he gave up his commendatory title to Boulogne, for which he had always a particular affection.[1] But the idea of becoming a religious had not yet entered his mind, at least not as a practical suggestion : that *horrible aversion* to the *frocard*, although weakened was not yet overcome.

He still wore his secular dress, and intended to lodge in the abbot's manse, as soon as it was rendered habitable. And it appeared to be his purpose to continue permanently in that position.

[1] Boulogne was donated to Henri de Barrillon, described by our Abbé as " the wisest and most virtuous priest in France." We shall meet him again as Bishop of Luçon.

There are indications, however, that he did not feel quite content with himself, that he felt himself called to something higher than the status of a conscientious commendatory abbot. "I find myself," he says in a letter dated September 17th, 1662, "animated with ardent desires to do penance, and nevertheless I am not doing it. I feel a poignant consciousness of my misery, and yet I pass my days in idleness. It seems that God would give me to understand that He desires only pure and perfect victims, and that I must leave myself in His hands as a lump of clay in the hands of the potter." Divine grace was stirring within him, urging him to yet another step in the ascent of his Calvary. What that step should be, he did not yet clearly know, but he must have had some suspicion. Anyhow, he was not left very long in doubt.

His relations with the religious left nothing to be desired. He treated them invariably with the utmost respect and consideration, envying them the innocence that gave them such favour with God. They, on their side, fairly idolised him for his patient kindness and sweet humility. They were constantly going to him for advice, and several had chosen him as the director of their conscience. One day a young religious, after making his confession, said to him : " Monsieur, I desire with all my heart that you would become the regular abbot of this community, instead of being what you are now, a mere commendatory superior. We should be very happy, I assure you, to have you for our master and guide in the way of salvation. It seems to me you have every qualification requisite for such a charge. I am not posing as a prophet, still I feel as certain as if I had an assurance from God, that my wishes in this matter will be one day fulfilled." " I am not worthy of so exalted an office," answered the Abbé, " but pray to God for me : nothing is impossible to His almighty power."

Some days afterwards, he had barely quitted the room he occupied in the abbatial manse when the ceiling came crashing down : had he been there he would almost certainly have been killed outright. He took this accident as an intimation that the abbot's lodge was not meant to be his residence.

The light was growing, but he did not yet see his way as clearly as he would wish. If God wanted him to remain in La Trappe, yet did not approve of his lodging in the apartments designed for the commendatory abbot, it appeared evident enough that the only place for him was in the ranks of the community ; still he decided to await a more direct manifestation of the Divine Will. It was not until the following year (1663) that his mind was fully enlightened. Whilst making his thanksgiving after Mass one day, to be precise, on April 17th, he entreated Our Lord, present in his heart, to make known to him in an unmistakable manner whether

he ought to be a monk, and if so, to give him the
courage and strength he would need in order to
conquer his repugnance to the monastic habit.
Just then he heard the religious, who were in choir
at the Office of Sext, chanting the verse : " They
that trust in the Lord shall be as Mount Sion, he
shall not be moved for ever that dwelleth in
Jerusalem " (Ps. cxxiv, 1). The words impressed
him as forcibly as if they had been addressed to him
directly by God in answer to his petition. They
flooded his soul with heavenly light and consolation,
leaving him as certain of his call to religion as he
was of his existence itself. He then and there made
up his mind definitely ; he put his hands to the
plough and would never look back.

A commendatory abbot could not change his
status for that of regular abbot without the royal
consent. So the Abbé had once again to repair to
Paris. His petition did not find favour with the
King's advisers. " His Majesty's interests are
involved," they answered him. " If all commendatory abbots acted in this way, the King would
be deprived of the means of rewarding his most
devoted servants." The Queen-Mother, Anne of
Austria, being appealed to, exerted her influence
in the Abbé's favour, with such happy results that
the King at last gave his sanction, yet " under this
condition, that on the death or resignation of the

Abbé de Rancé the aforesaid monastery of La
Trappe shall again become commendatory.''

An event that greatly rejoiced the Abbé at this
time was the entrance of his young niece, Louise-
Henriette d'Albon, into the Order of the Visitation.
Of all his relatives she seems to have been the
favourite. He wrote to her upwards of sixty letters
which breathe a tenderness of affection such as the
austere spirituality of most of his other writings
would hardly lead one to expect.

Whilst in Paris negotiating his change of status,
the Abbé learned that Dom Jouaud, Abbot of the
monastery of Prières, diocese of Vannes, Vicar-
General of the Reformed Cistercians, and one of
the holiest and most enlightened ecclesiastics of his
time, happened to be staying at the college of
St. Bernard in the same city. He went to inform
him of what he purposed to do. '' Father Abbot,''
he said, '' I have come to solicit of you the habit
of your Reform. I am a poor sinner who has need
of very austere penance, and I can see no other
way by which I may hope to return to God than
the way of the cloister. After so many disorders,
there is nothing left for me but to clothe myself
in sackcloth and offer to God the poor remains of
my wasted life, spending the rest of my days in
bitterness of heart.''

'' I do not think, Monsieur,'' replied the
Abbot, '' that you quite realise the meaning

of your request. You are a priest, a doctor
of the Sorbonne, a person of quality, brought up
in delicacy and luxury ; you are accustomed to
have a large retinue and to good cheer ; you are in
the way of being appointed to a bishopric ; your
health is anything but robust : and you want to
become a monk ! That is, you want to enter the
state which is the most abject, the most penitential,
the most obscure and the most despised in the
Church ! Henceforth, you will have to pass your
life in tears, in labour, in retirement, and to have
no other study than Jesus crucified. In fine, you
will have to renounce the world and all the pleasures
you have therein enjoyed. I beg of you, Monsieur,
think well of it."

" True, Father Abbot, I am a priest,"
answered the Abbè humbly, " but I have not
lived in a manner worthy of my calling. I have
been superior of several religious houses, but
instead of showing myself a father to the communities, I have squandered their property and the
patrimony of the Crucified. The ignorant gain
heaven by violence, and I with my doctorate and
my science, behold I perish, unless you will take pity
on me and grant me the favour I request. It is
true, I have made some figure in the world, but I
have been like one of those finger-posts which point
the right way to travellers without ever making a
move themselves. My resolution has been taken

not lightly but in prayer before God. Father Abbot, I desire to do penance. Please, don't refuse me."

There was no more opposition. "This is the finger of God," exclaimed the delighted Dom Jouaud, "He has inspired you with the purpose to become a monk. How can I resist His Will? No, but I will co-operate with your design to the very best of my power."

On his return to La Trappe, the Abbé found the religious still busy at the work of restoration. The old dormitory had fallen in, so that it had to be entirely rebuilt. Not knowing, at the time, the primitive practice of the Order, he caused separate cells to be made for the monks, which, later on, when he discovered his mistake, occasioned him many a worry and scruple. Only the thought of the expense it would entail prevented him from removing the cubicles and reverting to the original arrangement.

He was to make his noviciate in the abbey of Perseigne. On May 30th, the day preceding his departure from La Trappe, he wrote a very affectionate letter to one of his sisters in religion : "I believe God wishes me to consecrate the remainder of my poor life to the practice of penance, penance for having consecrated the better part thereof to the service of the world, and wishes me, moreover, to separate myself entirely from all intercourse with men. My regret is not to have known sooner His holy will, and to have rendered to the world that which I owed to my Creator. I am setting out to-morrow at break of day to begin my noviciate. I have great need of prayers, for, as you know, my perseverance rests in the hands of God. Entreat Him, I beg of you, to change my heart entirely. It is a comparatively easy matter to renounce external things, but how few there are who succeed in renouncing themselves !

" I shall never forget you, dear sister. You shall abide ever in my memory until we meet again in heaven where partings are no more. I beseech you once again : don't forget me in your prayers."

In the evening of the same day he summoned the whole community to the chapter-room, and announced to them his intention to pass the rest of his days amongst them, wearing the same habit and observing the same rule. The good religious wept tears of joy at this happy intelligence. Brother Bernier, who had been one of the original six, and by no means the most saintly, hearing that his beloved Abbé intended to go for his noviciate to Perseigne, threw himself at his feet and begged permission to accompany him. De Rancé was delighted beyond expression. It did not end there. The Abbé's valet, who had obstinately refused to part from him and had often and eloquently cursed the monks for spoiling such a sportsman with their prayers and penances and things, also begged leave to enter the noviciate with him. The permission, of course, was joyfully accorded. But it was some time before Brother Bernier could be spared at La Trappe.

CHAPTER IX.

Perseigne—De Rancé as a Novice—Illness—
Common and Strict Observance—Mission to
Champagne—Profession—Abbot of La Trappe
—Programme of Reform.

AT dawn on May 31st in the year of grace 1663,
the Abbè de Rancé and his faithful valet set out
from La Trappe and arrived at their destination in
the evening of the same day. Had they come as
ordinary visitors they would have received a warm
welcome, as St. Benedict's Holy Rule prescribes.
But as they came with the purpose of entering the
noviciate, they had to be treated in a different way,
in accordance with the prescriptions of the same
Holy Rule. " When any one presents himself at
the gate of the monastery begging admission into
the community, his request shall not be granted
until he shall have first been proved, according to
that of the Apostle : ' Try the spirits if they be of
God.' Wherefore, if the postulant continue to
knock at the gate for the space of four or five days,
and still persevere in his petition, notwithstanding
the affronts and humiliations to which he is
subjected, he shall be received and placed in the

guesthouse for a few days. He shall then enter the noviciate, where he is to take his meals, to sleep, and to apply himself to pious reading.'' It will be observed that there is no hint of such things as fatted calves or music and dancing to celebrate the prodigal's home-coming. However, St. Benedict knew what he was about. Only resolute souls, souls that have the courage to surmount his barricades and barbed wire entanglements, seemed in his eyes worthy to enter the Promised Land of the cloister. '' None but the brave deserve the fair '' prize of monastic peace.

According to custom, the two postulants were tried for a while in their secular dress, and received the habit together on June 13th, the feast of St. Antony, De Rancé being clad in the white of the choir religious, his valet—who took the name of Brother Antony—in the lay brother's brown. The Abbé himself retained his baptismal name, Armand-Jean. He found that rank and learning secured to their possessor no privileges at Perseigne. Quite the contrary. Such persons, being more likely than others to harbour sentiments of pride and self-sufficiency, have need of a more trying probation. Unless indeed we suppose, what was in truth the case, that the Abbé considered it a privilege to have assigned him the most abject and—according to merely human standards—degrading offices in the house.

He manifested now a more eager and insatiable avidity for sufferings and humiliations of every kind than he had ever shown in the world for honours and pleasures. The austerities prescribed by the Rule of St. Benedict and the constitutions of the Order only whetted his appetite for more. He was constantly applying to the master of novices for authorisation to inflict some fresh torment on mind or body. Having discovered that certain forms of mortification, used by the Cistercians of St. Bernard's day, had been long since given up as no longer practicable and did not even revive with the Reform, he gave the superiors no rest until he obtained permission to indulge in them. The other monks, ashamed to appear less mortified than he, followed his example, so that before he was many weeks in the house he had got well under way a new reform. A letter from Mgr. Pavillon, the austere Bishop of Aleth, in which the prelate highly approved of his entrance into religion and encouraged him to persevere, gave our zealous novice much consolation. "He addressed me in a manner so kindly," he wrote, " as to make it appear that I had really acted in accordance with the desire of his heart."

His bodily strength not being proportioned to his zeal and fervour, he suffered a bad breakdown in health towards the end of October, 1663. The illness had made alarming progress before his superiors knew anything about it, because he never complained. The physicians pronounced his life in danger, they attributed his malady to his imprudent mortifications ; even should they succeed in restoring his health it would be to little purpose unless he consented to return to the world, for the monastic life, they declared, was manifestly beyond his strength. When it was told him that his life could be saved only on condition of his abandoning the cloister, he answered calmly : '' Life is too dear at the price.'' In a letter to Mgr. Pavillon he says : '' I fell sick five months after my entrance into the noviciate ; but although the malady was very serious and brought me within a hair's breadth of dying, and was moreover according to all appearances the direct consequence of my change of life, God showed me such mercy that never for a moment did I feel the least temptation to abandon my purpose of spending the rest of my days in the cloister.''

However, the physicians insisted on his returning to La Trappe until his health was re-established. He remained there more than three months, that is, until the end of January. During his convalescence his friends used to bring him all kinds of delicacies, but nothing could induce him to accept anything of the sort, for he could not forget his resolution to live thenceforth only as a victim of expiation.

We have spoken more than once already of the

Reformed Cistercians and of the Cistercians of the Strict Observance. The two titles belonged to one and the same religious Congregation. But the reader will wonder if there was another class of Cistercians, Cistercians who were neither reformed nor strict. Yes, and the matter requires a little explanation which may conveniently be offered here.

The Cistercian Order was founded in the year of grace 1098 by SS. Robert, Alberic, and Stephen, and nineteen others, as a Benedictine Reform. The founders aimed at restoring the literal observance of St. Benedict's Holy Rule which in many points, of importance to their minds, had fallen into desuetude. At first it seemed as if the new Institute was destined to enjoy but a transient existence. No postulants presented themselves, and the members of the original community were going one after another to the grave. In the year 1112 St. Bernard and his companions found it at the point of extinction. But their advent infused new life into it. From that time it began to " increase and multiply and fill the earth." By the middle of the century, despite its austere observance, the new Order counted about 350 monasteries and nearly as many convents scattered throughout the whole of Christendom and inhabited by numerous and fervent communities. For 250 years the primitive austerity was well maintained. This period has deservedly been called the Golden Age, because

during these centuries the Cistercian Order supplied the history of monasticism with some of its most glorious chapters.

Then came the decadence. Many and various causes contributed to bring about the sad decline of fervour and discipline, but none so powerfully as the institution of commendatory abbots. During the fifteenth, sixteenth, and seventeenth centuries several attempts were made to revive the primitive austerity, but for one reason or another they met with only very partial success. The most important by far of these attempts must be considered that of the successor of St. Bernard, the devout Denis Largentier, Abbot of Clairvaux, who in the year 1615 introduced into his monastery much of the austere discipline (including perpetual abstinence and enclosure) that characterised the Order during the Golden Age. Other communities followed the example set by Clairvaux. Before long the Reform had found its way into no fewer than sixty-two monasteries and seven convents. The reformed houses grouped themselves into a Congregation, entitled the Congregation of the Strict Observance, subject, of course, to the jurisdiction of Citeaux, but with its own special constitutions and assemblies, and having a vicar-general at its head. At the time of De Rancé's noviciate this office was held by the Abbot of Prières, Dom Jean Jouaud. Those Cistercian communities that did not adopt the

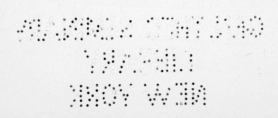

Reform came to be called the Cistercians of the
Common Observance. At their head stood the
Abbot of Citeaux, who was Superior-General of the
whole Order. During the period with which we are
now concerned, Citeaux had for abbot a man of
great influence in Church and State by reason of
his high birth and vast erudition, the celebrated
Claude Vaussin, to whose zeal and learning the
Cistercians owe, amongst other benefits, the reform
of their Breviary and Missal. An agreement had
been made between the two Observances with
regard to the extension of the disciplinary Reform.
It was this : if in any house the major part of the
community called for the introduction of that Reform, their desire should be satisfied. And that
brings us back to our story.

In the monastery of Champagne, diocese of
Mans, which had hitherto followed the Common
Observance, the majority of the religious had
recently declared in favour of introducing the Strict
Observance. Some of the Reformed Cistercians
were sent to assist in the undertaking. Now the
gentlemen of the neighbourhood did not at all relish
the idea of a change of discipline in the house ; it
would imply the loss of many of their privileges, the
right, for example, of entering the cloisters any
hour of the day or night. In concert with some
unworthy members of the community, they formed
the design of expelling by force the religious in

favour of the Reform. Tidings of the conspiracy came to the ears of the Perseigne superiors. What was to be done? An idea occurred to them. The Abbé de Rancé had been a great favourite with the country gentlemen in his hunting days : perhaps he could do something to prevent the threatened outrage. They asked him to go to Champagne, only a short distance away, and see if he could persuade those sacrilegious ruffians to abandon their design. He felt a great repugnance to undertaking such a mission ; he desired to forget the world altogether, and to prepare for his profession in tranquillity and recollection of soul. But of course obedience came before every other consideration. So he went, accompanied by another novice.

Hardly had he arrived at his destination when a troop of twenty-five armed horsemen, led by Marquis de Vassé, appeared before the monastery. Our novice sent a messenger to inform the Marquis that the Abbé de Rancé was in the house, and desired to have a word with him. The nobleman appeared thunder-struck at the news. Years before, the Abbé had been able to render him important service at court. He answered that he would go at once to De Rancé. He went with confusion on his countenance and tears in his eyes. It needed no eloquence to dissuade him from his purpose. The thought of a desecrated monastery and homeless, perhaps murdered monks could not have deterred him ; papal excommunications and royal proclamations he would have light-heartedly set at defiance. But he couldn't dream of resisting De Rancé. So the sentiment of gratitude is often found surviving the extinction of justice and the other virtues. The Marquis and his retainers went off in quest of other adventures : they never again molested the monks. After a few days' sojourn at Champagne, the Abbé and his companion returned to Perseigne whither the intelligence of their success had preceded them.

Some time afterwards it was proposed that he should proceed to Touraine on business somewhat similar to that which brought him to Champagne. His conscientious objections were so strong on this occasion that the matter was referred to the Vicar-General who decided in the novice's favour. Touraine was one of the places De Rancé had most reason to avoid.

The period of probation in the Cistercian, as in other monastic Orders, was then one year. St. Benedict himself considered that sufficient. As the time of his profession drew near the Abbé redoubled his fervour. All his pious friends were petitioned for the assistance of their prayers. The great boon he desired of God was a thorough conversion of heart. " I implore of you," he writes to Mgr. Pavillon, " to ask Almighty God for my conversion at the moment of this solemn act which is to be decisive of my eternity. Pray that, after having so often violated the vows of my baptism, I may have the grace to keep with fidelity the vows of religion which I am going to make." "As the hour approaches," he tells Mother Louise, "the desire to give myself irrevocably to God increases in intensity; and nevertheless I experience no diminution of my miseries. Still, the sense of my unworthiness, which I feel now more keenly than ever, produces nothing like discouragement. I put all my confidence in the goodness of my God; and I believe that His Providence, which has led me by the hand these seven years past, and did not abandon me even amid the disorders of my life in the world, will continue to watch over me now when I am possessed with such an ardent desire to be united with Him alone and for ever. Pray for my perseverance, I conjure you, and beg of the Lord to convert my heart entirely to Himself." Again, to the nuns of the Visitation at Tours : "Please all join in prayer for me. It is not enough to immolate oneself to God, it is further necessary to immolate oneself with the proper dispositions. You know the heavenly fire does not fall upon the sacrifice of those unhappy ones who offer to the Lord unclean victims. Not every kind of sacrifice is acceptable to Him. Be sure, then, to pray for my complete conversion."

A delay in the arrival of the necessary papers

necessitated the postponement of his profession. He felt grievously disappointed, but took it as part of his penance with entire submission to the holy Will of God. He had not long to wait, however. On June 19th the expected documents made their appearance, and the profession was fixed for the 26th of the same month.

The Abbé had always been distinguished for straight dealing and love of truth. Even when he was in the world and of the world it used to be said of him that he made a fetish of veracity. So now he felt obliged in conscience to make known to his superiors, on the very eve of his profession, something which, as he was well aware, might result in their refusing to receive his vows. He had formed the resolution, if professed, to revive in his monastery of La Trappe the primitive observance of Citeaux in all its rigour; and he would only pronounce his vows on the understanding that he should be left at liberty to carry out his design. This announcement greatly embarrassed the superiors at Perseigne. They tried to reason with him. The Strict Observance, they said, included all that was of moment in the primitive observance, it was as much as human nature could endure, the heroic penance of St. Bernard's time would never again be possible. But they argued in vain. The Abbé continued resolute. There was nothing for it, then, but to refer the question to the Vicar-General.

I

Again, this prelate gave his verdict in De Rancé's favour.   Doubtless he recognised that the Abbé was acting under some special inspiration of the Holy Ghost. So on June 26th, 1664, Armand-Jean le Bouthillier de Rancé, Master of Arts and Doctor of the Sorbonne, with this understanding, pronounced his vows of poverty, chastity, obedience, stability, and conversion of manners, according to the prescription of St. Benedict's Rule and the traditions of the Cistercian Order.

Along with him were professed two other novices, both destined like himself for La Trappe. On the day following his profession he requested a friend of his, Canon Félibien of Chartres, to proceed to La Trappe and in his name take formal possession of the abbey. According to the canons then in force, a commendatory abbot became regular abbot by the fact of profession, although he still required the abbatial benediction. The right of election did not exist.

Three days after his profession the Abbé wrote as follows to Mother Louise :

" This note is to confirm your anticipation that I am now a professed monk. I made my vows three days ago, so that I am now bound to God for the rest of my life in a state which has always appeared to me, judging by earthly standards, extremely vile and contemptible, hence very appropriate for a man like me who has to perform penance for his sins. Do you ask what were my interior sentiments at the moment of profession? I will tell you briefly. I saw myself as one condemned to the fires of hell on account of the heinousness and multitude of his sins, and I felt convinced at the same time that the only way to appease the just anger of God was to consecrate myself to a practice of penance that shall only end with my life. Yet I know not if my penance will please Him, if the public satisfaction which I am resolved to make henceforth will be acceptable in His eyes. But this much I do know : that I have knocked at the only door which was open to me, and that it is only through the same I can hope to enter into the peace of Jesus Christ. I quite understand all the reasons for doubting that the mercy of God would extend even to miseries and disorders so great as mine ; nevertheless, in spite of all, I am full of hope, and God has given me such confidence that I abandon myself blindly to His Providence. I leave the decision of my eternal destiny altogether in His hands. I shall strive my best to keep inviolably with most constant fidelity the vows which my heart has made to Him a thousand times before my lips pronounced them. It is my greatest consolation to think that I serve a Master Who never abandons such as persevere to the last in His service. He is the Lord : let Him do what is good in His sight. None has the right to complain of His ordinances. As for me, I shall do my duty always, or at least I shall always pray for the grace to do so. Such, in short, have been and are still my dispositions : complete resignation to the Providence of God and abandonment of myself to His holy Will. I remember to have read in St. John Climacus that a person who has been so unhappy as to lose the grace of God ought never to put a stop to the flow of his tears until he has heard directly from God Himself or from one of His angels that all his sins have been blotted out.''

The ceremony of blessing the new Abbot was deferred until July 13th. All the time intervening De Rancé spent in retreat, for he regarded the abbatial benediction as a solemn consecration of himself to the task of promoting the spiritual interests of his community, and therefore desired to approach it with the best dispositions possible. It was expected that the function would take place at La Trappe. But in order to avoid the concourse of his friends and relatives, he preferred to have it in some monastery where he would be almost a stranger. Hence he made choice of Saint Martin's, in the diocese of Seez, a house belonging to the Benedictine Congregation of St. Maur. The officiating prelate was Mgr. Patrick Plunkett, the exiled Bishop of Ardagh, formerly Abbot of the Cistercian monastery known as St. Mary's, Dublin, and uncle to the martyred Primate, Blessed Oliver. Next day the Abbot de Rancé, as we shall entitle him henceforth, took the road to La Trappe.

On the third day after his arrival he received the profession of a novice. The novice was none other than his quondam valet, now Brother Antony. This religious, as we have said, made his noviciate at Perseigne with his master, but such was his affection for De Rancé that he postponed the taking of his vows until he should have the consolation of taking them in his presence and under his authority. The ceremony took place at La Trappe, July 18th. On the same day all the professed religious of the community solemnly renewed their vows and promised obedience to their new Abbot.

De Rancé was no sooner installed at the head of his community than he showed he had neither abandoned nor forgotten the grand design, formed during his noviciate, to revive the primitive observance in La Trappe. The regime hitherto followed in this house—that is, since its restoration—was that of Perseigne and the other houses of the Reformed Cistercians. Estimated in accordance with the standards of that time, it certainly seemed austere enough. The monks observed perpetual abstinence from flesh meat, but had good substitutes in fish and eggs, wine also was permitted in limited quantity. They kept the monastic fasts in addition to those prescribed by the common law of the Church, but even on fast days they dined at 11 a.m., and had collation in the evening. They rose at 2 a.m. for the Offices of Matins and Lauds, but they retired to rest again when these Offices were over. They practised silence, but were allowed an hour's recreation after dinner. The law of enclosure was strictly enforced, but visitors had no difficulty in obtaining interviews with the monks, and there was a long walk for the community every week. Again, there seems to have been no restriction on letter-writing, and manual labour had in great degree fallen into desuetude, the time formerly devoted thereto being now given to study. Abbot de Rancé had definitely made up his mind to allow nothing in La Trappe that he thought St. Bernard would discountenance. He could find no justification for the above-mentioned indulgences in the practice of the Cistercians of St. Bernard's day; therefore they would find no toleration at La Trappe.

Nevertheless he exercised the utmost prudence and circumspection in the carrying out of his design. He did not employ his authority for the purpose, but relied altogether on the lure of his personal example and the power of his exhortation. It was thus he induced the community to give up the use of wine. Other sacrifices, too, they would be asked to make, but not immediately. "He never made use of his authority as Abbot," writes Dubois, "to establish any of those observances which a fervour, always fresh and strong, has kept up without intermission to our times. Far from being an imperious, self-sufficient autocrat, whenever there was question of introducing new regulations or practices he invariably consulted his brethren—so he always called his monks. And as if he were himself devoid of all wisdom and experience, he would condescend to ask the advice of the youngest member of the community. Sometimes, by studied delays, he would make the religious impatient for that which he in reality desired the most ardently of all ; and he would only yield to their reiterated and most urgent solicitations." How does this compare with the autocratic, draconian character given him by the prattling M. Bremond ?

It favoured De Rancé's purpose as a reformer that the community of La Trappe was not very numerous at the time he took charge of it. At his return in July, 1664, it numbered only ten, including two novices. They were all very fervent. He could, therefore, entertain the hope of being able to win over to his views those who had already made profession under the old regime, and with regard to the novices, he could refuse to receive to profession all that were unwilling to live like the monks of the Golden Age. The programme looked simple. The only matter in doubt was this : would the austerity of the discipline he purposed to introduce frighten good subjects away ? The same doubt, he remembered, presented itself to the mind of the founders of Citeaux. And he determined to show himself not less courageous, not less trustful in Providence than they. If God approved of his undertaking, and he felt certain He did, He would not fail to inspire true vocations and the courage to act up to them ; if He did not approve, well then the sooner his design came to nothing the better.

CHAPTER X.

De Rancé appointed Champion of the Strict Observance—Journey to Rome—Cardinal Bona — Discouragement — Interview with Abbot Vaussin—Audience with Alexander VII—Commission appointed—Pilgrimage to Subiaco.

In a letter dated August 8th, 1664, Abbot de Rancé tells a friend : " In truth my attraction for solitude is so great that everything which withdraws me therefrom makes me suffer keenly. And I know from experience that external occupations, even such as are directed to the glory of God, produce, nevertheless, much distraction of mind. How happy should I be if I could live as much aloof from commerce with human affairs as if I belonged to another world ! This I have often said, but never before have I been so convinced of its truth. Hence I feel a most ardent desire to be as completely forgotten by men as if I had never existed." Is not this St. Bernard's *ama nesciri,* " love to be unknown and accounted for nothing," as the Imitation paraphrases it ? But the pious Abbot's desire for solitude was not to be satisfied yet awhile. At this very time the already old controversy between the two Observances began again, and he was about to be dragged into the maelstrom.

Towards the end of August Abbot de Rancé received a letter from the Abbot of Prières, Vicar-General of the Reformed Cistercians, summoning him to a conference of the superiors of the Congregation which would open in the college of St. Bernard, Paris, on September 1st. Reluctantly, and simply as an exercise of obedience to legitimate authority, he quitted La Trappe and set out for the capital. He expected that the business on hand would detain him from home for no more than a couple of weeks at the longest. Vain hope ! Thirty-two abbots attended the conference. The purpose of the meeting was to select deputies to be sent to Rome to defend there the interests of the Strict Observance. Pope Alexander VII, who dearly loved the Cistercian Order, and seemed to have made it the ambition of his life to bestow on it again the blessings of concord and unity, had requested that both Observances should send representatives to the Curia to see whether terms of adjustment could not be found. The conference at St. Bernard's resulted in the choice of Abbot de Rancé and Abbot Dominique Georges, superior of Du Val Richer, a man eminent for prudence, learning, and holiness of life. De Rancé did all in his power to convince his brother-abbots of his utter unfitness for a mission of this kind. He represented

the incongruity of sending a man of his antecedents
to plead their cause at Rome, the dangers to which
he would be exposed, his inexperience and ignorance
of monastic life, and in particular his reluctance to
absent himself for so long from his little family at
Our Lady of La Trappe. All his objections were
overruled. The common good should prevail over
private interests. He, with his learning, his
eloquence, his zeal, his courage and prestige, was
the person best qualified to uphold the cause of the
Reformers, and he should go as the principal deputy.
That left nothing more to be said, so he submitted,
although with pain and disquietude, as to the manifest Will of God.

The superiors of the Reform were so poor that
they could not provide the funds necessary to
defray the expenses of the journey to Rome. De
Rancé undertook to collect the money. It was his
intention to beg it of his wealthy friends in the
world, although the very thought of such a thing
must have been agony to his sensitive nature.
Providence, however, spared him this humiliation.

As the preparation of the memorials which the
deputies were to present to the Holy See would
occupy some time, Abbot de Rancé determined to
spend that interval in his own monastery. So,
immediately after the conference he returned to La
Trappe. He found on his arrival that Brother
Bernier, who, like himself, had gone to Perseigne

for his noviciate, but two months later, had now come back, his probation completed. The Abbot received his profession on September 18th. This religious, once so wild that he " neither feared God nor regarded man," was now a model of all Christian and monastic virtues. He possessed an exceedingly beautiful voice, so that people used to come from all parts to hear him singing the praises of God. For many years he occupied the position of cantor in the choir at La Trappe.

That was not the only consolation prepared for the Abbot during this short visit home. One day whilst he was busily employed at manual work with his community, reclaiming a piece of land that had been long neglected, rain began to fall. The prior suggested the advisibility of his seeking shelter. " Such delicacy does not become poor penitents," answered the Abbot, digging his spade into the ground. The implement struck on something hard. Thinking it was a stone, he dug it out and found that the resisting object was a fairly large metal box filled with old English crowns. Other similar pieces were discovered in the earth around the casket. The total value of the find came to about five hundred francs. This, with what the procurator of the monastery could spare, would suffice to cover the expenses of the journey to Rome. The incident comforted De Rancé less by the great convenience

it meant for him than by the assurance it gave that
Divine Providence was still watching over him.

All too soon the day arrived when he had again
to take the road to Paris. He took a most affectionate leave of his religious, embracing them one
by one, and soliciting the help of their prayers. On
his arrival in the capital, he approached many of
his influential friends for letters of recommendation
that might facilitate matters at the Curia. Bremond
has an ignorant gibe at this display of worldly
prudence, forgetting that De Rancé was surely in
good company here. Letters were procured from
the Queen-Mother, the Duchess de Orleans, the
Duchess de Longueville, Prince de Conti, Cardinal
de Retz, and more than thirty members of the
French episcopate. Some were addressed to the
Pope himself, others to the officials of his court ;
all testified to the esteem in which the clergy and
people of France held the Cistercians of the Strict
Observance.

But the Common Observance had its supporters
too, and supporters more numerous and powerful
than those of the Reform. That need not surprise
us. What does surprise us is to find men of equal
sanctity, prudence, zeal, and learning ranged on
opposite sides. Of the two party leaders, Abbot
Vaussin of Citeaux merited to be praised for his
piety by M. Olier, and Abbot Jouaud of Prières was
probably as good a religious as could then be found

in Christendom. And the question which so hope-
lessly divided them? It looks small enough to our
eyes, much smaller than the question of concord
and peace. In short, the Cistercians of the Strict
Observance desired to impose their Reform on the
whole Order, at least so far as the perpetual abstinence from flesh meat. Until they had succeeded in
this, they claimed the right to have their own
particular rules, their own assemblies, their own
vicar-general, whilst remaining nominally subject to
the jurisdiction of the Abbot of Citeaux. That right
had been acknowledged, and was embodied in the
status quo at the time of De Rancé's entrance into
the Order. Now, however, the party of the Common
Observance demanded the suppression of their
opponents' rules, assemblies and vicar-general, as
tending to produce a schism in the Cistercian
Institute. There was undoubtedly a great deal to
be said for both sides—a great deal *was* said, much
more than was necessary—but, as usual, in the
heat of the controversy zealous partizans could only
be brought to see the case for their own side, or
rather they felt convinced that theirs was the only
side.

The Pope sincerely desired to satisfy both
parties—not an easy thing to do even for a
Sovereign Pontiff, their claims being diametrically
opposed. But his sympathies seemed to have been
enlisted on the side of the Reformers. Certainly

nothing would have pleased him better than to behold the children of St. Bernard walking again, as one united body, in the way their holy Father had traced out for them. At the same time he did not believe that this result, in itself so desirable, could or should be brought about by means of legislation. If the religious of the Common Observance would voluntarily renounce the privileges and dispensations granted them by his predecessors or legitimated by custom, well and good ; but if they declined to do this, he could not see his way to force them. The conference to be held in Rome represented the final effort of his zeal for unity.

September 28th, the day before his leaving Paris for Rome, Abbot de Rancé wrote as follows to his community at La Trappe : " I pray Our Lord to fill your hearts with His Holy Spirit. I could not begin my journey without employing the few moments at my disposal to testify to you once more that nothing in the world could have caused me greater grief than this separation, and that never before has God so clearly manifested to me as at this hour what a force of affection for you He has put into my heart. My only consolation comes from the thought that, in sacrificing all the inclinations and sentiments of my heart by the blind obedience I render to the orders of my superiors, I may hope to merit His all-powerful protection both for you and for myself. Be assured, my dearest brethren, that I shall bear you all in the very centre of my heart. At all times and in every place, but especially at the foot of the crucifix, I shall be mindful of you to whom by the grace of God I am so warmly attached. I implore of Jesus Christ to re-live in each of you His own life of penance, whereby he appeased His Father's anger justly enkindled against men. And I exhort you to abandon yourselves to Him and to regard His love as the one thing worth living for. To this you are indispensably obliged by your profession. Without this absolute abandonment of yourselves into the hands of God, your religion would be vain, and your penance, full of illusions, would yield neither the fruit nor the recompense you expect from it. I am so hurried that I have only time to place before your eyes these words of St. Bernard : ' My children, if you only knew how great are the obligations of a monk, you would never eat a morsel of bread without watering it with your tears.' Pray for me, and remember that my salvation and yours are inseparably bound together according to the order of Divine Providence. On my side, I shall beg of God to show mercy to you as to myself, and to shower upon you His graces and blessings. And as He has separated us for a while may He be pleased to reunite us for ever."

At Châlons he was joined by his confrère, Abbot Dominique Georges, and also by his friend, Canon

Félibien, who desired to accompany him to Rome.
Passing through Lyons, he availed of the opportunity to visit the chapel of the Visitation where is
preserved the heart of St. Francis de Sales. He
was permitted to kiss that sacred relic, which he
accounted a great privilege. On the way over the
Alps he met with what almost proved to be a fatal
accident. A sudden gust of wind blew him off his
horse, and he came within an ace of being swept
over the brink of a precipice which bordered the
road. When he realised how narrow had been his
escape, his first thought and act was to return
thanks to the Almighty for His never-failing protection. At Turin he and his companions were met
by the French ambassador and conducted to the
presence of Charles Emanuel II, who treated the
Abbot of La Trappe with the greatest respect. This
Prince had lately married the Duke of Orleans'
daughter, an old friend of De Rancé's. The
travellers had the consolation of venerating the Holy
Winding-Sheet before they departed from the city.

At Milan they prayed before the tomb of St.
Charles Borromeo, and visited the garden where of
old St. Augustine, fighting the last terrible fight
against his passions, heard the mysterious words :
Tolle, lege; tolle, lege. The scene made a profound impression on De Rancé's mind. It recalled
to him another garden and another, yet similar,
struggle fought out to a like victorious issue beneath

the skies of Touraine. He knelt before the bodies
of SS. Dominic and Catherine at Bologna.   At
Florence the Grand Duke Ferdinand II received
him with as much honour as if he were a prince of
the blood and loaded him with gifts, which were
promptly transferred to the hospital for the benefit
of the poor.

The Abbot of La Trappe and his travelling companions arrived in Rome on November 14th, six
weeks after leaving Paris. The letters they brought
secured them a welcome from many of the Roman
notabilities. But none received them with so much
cordiality as the illustrious scholar, Cardinal Bona,
who was himself a Cistercian, and strongly in favour
of the Reform. He warned the deputies, however,
that their mission was foredoomed to failure : the
most powerful personages in the courts of Rome
and France were opposed to the reforming party ;
indeed the only important protector the party
possessed was the Queen-Mother, Anne of Austria,
and her death, which could not now be very far
off, would mean in all probability the death of the
Strict Observance.

" What !" exclaimed De Rancé.   " Do you
mean to say that the court of Rome could resolve
to destroy an Observance established by the
authority of the Holy See itself in more than sixty
monasteries which are the edification of France,
without counting the convents of nuns ?   Where

then shall piety, virtue, and penance find protection if not with the Pope?"

"Softly, my dear Abbé," answered the Cardinal, taking both the other's hands in his own, "here in Italy people do not speak so loud. The Pope is very well disposed towards the Reform; he loves everything good and virtuous. I will even venture to promise that you will have a gracious reception from him, because the Bishop of Evreux has informed him of your merits. So he is expecting you. But the misfortune is that his health is declining day by day, he rarely grants audiences, and Cardinal Chigi, his nephew, who has no sympathy with your cause, has obtained control of everything. Make haste, therefore. I will go and endeavour to arrange an immediate audience for you with his Holiness."

Whilst awaiting the hour when they would be summoned to the audience-chamber, the two deputies interviewed a number of cardinals and other persons of consequence. Discouragement on every side! They met with no lack of politeness and charity, but when it came to the question of the Reform people said to them as if the matter had already been decided: "After all, God requires only the heart; He does not want us to destroy our bodies; it is a thing of small consequence whether one does or does not abstain from flesh meat; above all things, one must submit one-

self to the ruling of the Holy See." Evidently
Abbot Vaussin of Citeaux, who had come to Rome
a month earlier than his opponents, had not been
wasting his time. Yes, Cardinal Bona was right :
they must abandon all hope of securing a favourable
verdict. They had even cause to fear the total
abolition of the Reform as the only means of re-
establishing concord and peace in the Cistercian
Institute. Such, as they well knew, was the
demand of Abbot Vaussin and his friends.

Alarmed at the prospect, De Rancé determined to
offer an accommodation—to save something since it
was not possible to save everything. He called upon
the Abbot of Citeaux, and after speaking of the desirableness of avoiding scandal, which would be
inevitable if their difference went before the public
tribunals, he made the following proposal : His
party would cease from their endeavours to impose
their Observance on the whole Order, they would
continue to recognise the Abbot of Citeaux as their
head and to attend the General Chapters held in his
monastery, he on his side should guarantee that they
would be permitted to live in their own way un-
molested, to retain their vicars-general (confirmed
by him) and their particular assemblies.

" You desire, then, to create a schism in the
Order ?" said Vaussin.

" There can be no question of schism," answered
De Rancé, " where all acknowledge the same head,

even though all do not wear the same uniform. Otherwise we should have to pronounce the whole Church in schism. The arrangement I propose is the one actually adopted in the Orders of St. Francis and St. Dominic.''

Abbot Vaussin appeared to be somewhat impressed. He said he could not then give a definite answer, but would consider the suggestion. Two days after he visited De Rancé at his lodgings, and told him that if the spokesmen of the Reform had all been as courteous and moderate as he had shown himself, the dispute would have been quickly settled, but now the case was in the hands of the Holy See, and they must be satisfied to await its decision : he had himself promised the Pope to introduce a reform throughout the entire Order, and one that would give pleasure to his Holiness. The Abbot of La Trappe was about to reply, but was prevented by the entrance of the Bishop of Evreux. The opportunity did not offer again. He did not find much consolation in the thought of a general reform originating from Citeaux : he knew only too well what it would mean : the Common Observance would be levelled up just a little, the Strict Observance would be levelled down rather more. And the Strict Observance at its best fell so far short of St. Bernard's practice, so far short of his own ideal !

On December 2nd the deputies of the Reform

assisted at the Pope's Mass, after which they were admitted to audience. Alexander received them with more than his ordinary graciousness. The Abbot of La Trappe made him an address in beautiful Latin, protesting his absolute submission to the authority of the Holy See whose judgment he would receive with as much respect as if it proceeded from the mouth of Christ Himself. He then went on to speak of the decadent condition of the Cistercian Order, once the brightest ornament of the Church, of the efforts made in France to restore to it something of its ancient splendour, and of the determined opposition those efforts were encountering. The entire Church mourned over the fall of Citeaux, "but at the news that your Holiness, heir to Christ's pastoral vigilance not less than to His supreme authority, has taken in hand the task of effecting a thorough reform, a task so worthy of your solicitude, she has shaken off her sadness, she has dried her tears, and rejoices now in the assured hope that the Institute of Citeaux has not only reached the term of its misfortunes, but is about to recover the lustre of its prime. The high reputation for wisdom which you, Holy Father, so deservedly enjoy throughout Christendom does not permit us to doubt the success of your enterprise. That success is the hope of the Church, the expectation of kingdoms and peoples. The importance of the matter keeps all minds in suspense, all eyes directed to the

pontifical throne. We might have been certain of
obtaining much from St. Gregory the Great, who
was so devoted to the Order of St. Benedict : we
can look for no less to Alexander, who is equally
great, who by the fervour of his piety, by the
beauty of his soul, by the renown of his wisdom,
measures fully up to the level of the greatest of his
predecessors. It only remains to solicit one favour
of your Holiness—if it is permitted. The favour
is this : considering the gravity of the affair, the
great hopes entertained by the whole world, the
desirableness of making a thorough investigation and
of accrediting the Reform which is about to be
established and introduced into so many different
and such remote nations, we pray your Holiness to
entrust this task to a commission of cardinals of
the Holy Roman Church.''

The Pope listened to the speech with great
attention. In reply he assured the deputies of his
esteem for the Reformed Cistercians whose progress
in France he had watched with much satisfaction ;
he would be glad to see the Strict Observance
adopted by the whole Order ; his sentiments in this
matter he had made known to the Abbot of Citeaux,
and had refused to come to any decision until he
had seen the representatives of both parties ; finally
he promised his protection to the Reform.

Before leaving the audience chamber De Rancé
solicited a special blessing for his abbey of La

Trappe. He had every reason to feel satisfied with the result of the interview. His hopes mounted still higher when he learned a few days later that Alexander, true to his word, had already appointed a Commission of cardinals to examine the questions in dispute between the two Observances.

During the Christmas season the Commission suspended its sessions ; and taking advantage of this interval the two deputies of the Reform made a pilgrimage to Subiaco, the hallowed spot where their holy Father and legislator, St. Benedict, passed three years in silence and solitude. Contemplating the scene of his lonely penance, they renewed their determination to leave no means untried to restore to their Order the Strict Observance of the Holy Rule.

CHAPTER XI.

An Untoward Event—Findings of the Commission—
De Rancé leaves Rome—His Return—Letter to
Mother Louise—Cardinal Bona Again—Trouble
in La Trappe—De Rancé's Relatives complain
of Him—The Deputies have a second Audience
with Alexander—Return to France.

THE Commission, although not likely to satisfy the
Reformers in every particular, would almost
certainly have imposed the obligation of perpetual
abstinence on the whole Order but for an unfortunate incident that occurred just then at the Sorbonne. A professed choir religious of Perseigne, defending a thesis for his baccalaureate before the university, upheld the views of the Gallican theologians
against the opinions favourable to the authority of the
Holy See. The Vicar-General of the Strict Observance was present, but instead of imposing silence on
his subject appears to have joined in the applause.
To make matters worse, a memorial presented to the
French Monarch by the Reformed Cistercians was
found to have a very decided savour of Gallicanism.
The Papal Nuncio in Paris promptly transmitted
these facts to the Curia. The result was that the

Roman diplomats and officials began to look with suspicion on all supporters of the Reform, as if all were to be held accountable for the act of a few. This suspicion influenced the deliberations on the issue of which the fate of the Reform depended. On January 20th it was proposed to decree the suppression of the Strict Observance with all that it stood for. " I have read a copy of the decree," Cardinal Bona told De Rancé, " it has been presented to the Holy Father who has had the goodness to send it to me for examination. It is directed against the Reform. I have made a good many changes, and I have softened it as much as was possible. But I cannot promise you that my alterations will be allowed to stand. It is a grievous disappointment, in truth, and I feel it more deeply than words can express."

" How different are the counsels of God from those of men !" exclaimed the Abbot. " Who would have believed that an institution so edifying, so holy, as the Strict Observance is about to be destroyed, and destroyed by the same authority to which it owes its existence ? Where now shall we find solid foundations on which we can build with security ?" The tears were in his eyes as he spoke. " I cannot believe," he added, " that His Holiness wishes to destroy the Reform, after all the assurances he gave me of his special protection, even of his friendship and esteem. I must see him again."

He asked for another audience, but did not obtain it ; the Pope's state of health would not permit his attending to business matters ; the Abbot must address himself to the Commission entrusted with his case. He knew then that the cause was lost beyond remedy. In his humility he regarded the misfortune as a visitation on his past sins, and wrote to the Vicar-General to that effect. Just when he had abandoned all hope of saving the Reform, succour came to him from an unexpected quarter. The Queen-Mother of France sent a strong letter to the Commission testifying to her admiration for the Strict Observance and her deep interest in its prosperity, and letting the fact appear that she had taken it under her special protection. This so much impressed the minds of the cardinals concerned that they considered it more advisable to proceed no further for the present, and to postpone the publication of the fatal decree : they did not expect that the Queen-Mother would live very long.

As soon as De Rancé came to understand the position of affairs, he consulted judicious friends as to what course of conduct he would do best to adopt. " Under the circumstances," they counselled, " you will serve your cause best by retiring from the city." It may be that they thought him a little in the way, on account of his incurable candour. The art of dissembling was not included in the long and varied list of his accomplishments.

Anyhow, he received their advice with the greatest satisfaction. He could not see what benefit to the cause could be expected from his stay in Rome ; besides he was hungering for the solitude and peace of his beloved monastery. So on February 4th, 1665, he left the Eternal City, resolved to place all his confidence thenceforth in God alone, " for vain is the help of man."

At his arrival in Lyons he found a number of letters awaiting him. The contents of nearly all were alike in character : remonstrances and re-proaches, and even abuse. *Quo vadis?* Was he fleeing like a craven from the cross ? He had betrayed the cause, the writers complained, he had deserted his post ; if the Reform should be sup-pressed the responsibility would lie with him. We can imagine what pain such cruel criticism caused one so sensitive as De Rancé. Not all his corres-pondents, however, showed themselves so unkind. Abbot Jouaud, the Vicar-General, expressed regret at his action indeed, but with the utmost gentleness. At the same time he requested him for the sake of the cause they both had so much at heart to return immediately to Rome were his services would be needed very soon : Cardinal de Retz was going in person to the Curia to second his efforts there, whilst the Queen-Mother and other powerful friends were about to make a direct appeal to the Pope on their behalf. All sick and weary though he was, and despite the inclemency of the weather—it was the month of February—he turned on his road and hastened back to the metropolis which he hoped he had seen the last of.

In a letter to his friend, Mother Louise of the Visitation, he refers to the incident as follows : — " I perceive by your letter that you have suffered a good deal on my account, and that you are much concerned for the interests of my reputation. My action in leaving Rome has been differently interpreted by different persons. Those who feel neither friendship nor goodwill for me have put an uncharitable construction upon it. That, of course, is only what I should expect. Nevertheless, the interests of our cause, and the condition of things, which was then decidedly unfavourable to us, obliged me to that course. Neither passion nor caprice had anything to do with it. Moreover, the suggestion did not come from myself. but from persons of the highest reputation for wisdom, to whose judgment I merely deferred. . . . . Nevertheless, when I received from my superiors the order to return to Rome, although illness and fatigue and the severity of the season furnished a legitimate excuse for delaying, I began to retrace my steps immediately. I may tell you that all the cardinals and others with whom I have to deal welcomed me back with every demonstration of joy—which pleased me very much. In deference to my wishes, they have postponed giving judgment on our affairs until the arrival of Cardinal de Retz, who is expected within three or four days. I don't know what the result will be. I can assure you, however, that I have not shown any hastiness in the conduct of this business, nor do I remember to have said one single word that could be regarded as unbecoming a person of my calling. I have spoken strongly when the occasion required it, and under the like circumstances I shall do so again. But you must not be surprised if, having enemies at Rome due to the cause which Divine Providence has given me to sustain, I should be misrepresented and my actions severely criticised. Although my desire for solitude is stronger than ever, I shall never, by the mercy of God, take a single step to procure it so long as obedience requires me to remain in the world. It was for the sake of Jesus Christ that I exchanged the world for the desert, and now I should be very unfaithful if I refused for His sake to exchange the desert for the world. We are quite safe wherever we are, provided His Will has placed us there.''

M. Bremond takes occasion of this '' flight '' of De Rancé from Rome to air a little more of his precious psychology. According to his view, the Abbot was a coward at heart who occasionally, under stress of excitement and a longing for the limelight, used to frighten himself into panic with spectacular displays of courage, or what looked

like it. And he has the brazen impudence to give
the lie direct to the holy religious. De Rancé says
he left Rome by the advice of his friends, for the
best interests of his cause, which he believed his
sins were prejudicing. Nonsense, exclaims the
Academician. *Credat judaeus, non ego* : tell that
to your apologists, like this credulous Dubois. You
really left Rome as you left the General Assembly
in Paris from sheer terror. There is no use in trying
to deck your cowardly conduct '' in holy colours.''
What he had to fear either at Rome or in Paris
M. Bremond does not trouble to explain.

All the time that he spent outside his monastery,
the Abbot lived according to the regime of La
Trappe without the least relaxation, no matter
where he was or the work he had to do. He took so
little food and rest that his friends became alarmed
and reported the matter to his superiors. The
result of this was an order from the Vicar-General
to moderate his austerities and to submit in this
matter to the direction of his colleagues—Abbot
Dominque Georges and Cardinal de Retz : they
would be his superiors in all that concerned his
health.

In the month of August of the same year, 1665,
he received disquieting news from La Trappe.
Despite all his preaching about unity and concord,
it was now a house divided against itself ! Before his
departure from the monastery he had given minute

instructions to his prior, Father John Gauthier, relative to the discipline of the house, but said nothing that would seem to authorise the introduction of any new austerities. So far the only change the Abbot had made with regard to diet was the exclusion of wine from the refectory ; he had indeed expressed the desire to see the religious dispensing with fish and eggs also, but as yet he had never asked them to do this. In his absence, therefore, the prior continued to have these articles of food served at dinner. Several members of the community, including the sub-prior, objected, and accused him of acting against the known will of the Abbot. The Vicar-General was called in to decide the question, but was unable to restore peace. Then he suggested (what should have been done at the beginning) that they should write to Abbot de Rancé and thus find out what his intention was.

" I cannot tell you how pained I was," wrote the Abbot on August 20th, " to hear that our house has not persevered in that state of peace, union and concord which it ought to have, and which I hoped it would maintain during my absence. You would understand the poignancy of my grief, if you knew how I bear you all in the very centre of my heart, so that nothing touches me so intimately as that which concerns you ; and you are as much my preoccupation whilst I am here in Rome as you were when I was in the monastery. . . . . You know, my dear brethren, that your penance cannot please God unless it be accompanied with true charity and sincere humility. Works that are dead cannot be acceptable to the Living God."

Some weeks after the date of this letter his married sister, Madame de Vernassel, died in Auvergne at the age of forty. It then became known that Abbot de Rancé, in disposing of his possessions in the interests of religion and the poor, had deprived her and other of his relatives of property they believed themselves entitled to. This raised another violent storm against him. " I have reason to rejoice," he told a correspondent, October 15th, " but only according to the superior part of my soul. God is treating me as He treats those whom He loves with a love of predilection. All my relatives seem to have the same bad opinion of me. Yesterday I received a letter from Madame le Bouthillier which would surprise you. . . . . God is very good to have thus opened to me the ways which have sanctified His elect. But that is not enough, unless He also gives me the grace to walk in those ways with constant fidelity. Please, pray for me that I may deserve to obtain what I need so much. With regard to the disposition I have made of my property, I considered that, in this matter, I was obliged to act according to the rules of conscience rather than according to the opinions of those who measure everything by their own interests. Let me tell you also that, since my withdrawal from the world, I have so abandoned my reputation to the judgments of men that it has never occurred to me to attempt to justify myself in their eyes. He who awaits in fear the judgment of Jesus Christ makes but small account of what men think of him.''

Meantime, the negotiations at Rome relative to the two Observances continued to drag their slow length along. We shall not weary the reader with the details. The death of the Queen-Mother, Anne of Austria, January 20th, 1666, deprived the Reformers of their last hope.

Abbot de Rancé, faced with the certain prospect of having to abandon his cherished design to live according to the primitive observance of the Holy Rule, and at the same time feeling called to a life of austere penance, resolved to apply for permission to pass from the Institute of Citeaux to that of Chartreuse. The permission was granted, subject, however, to the condition that he should find it impossible to live at La Trappe as his conscience directed. '' God is admirable in all His ways,'' he wrote, '' He hides from our view what our weakness could not support, and ordinarily His Providence puts us in those places and in those states the bare thought of which beforehand would have terrified us. I suffer more than I can tell in the position in which He has placed me. All its circumstances are painful to me, and the only thing that renders it at all endurable is the assurance implied in the very repugnance I feel that it is not my own will I am following but the Will of God. . . . . The bitterness of the chalice presented to us is nearly always a reason for accepting it, but can never be a legitimate reason for refusing it."

There being now no reason for prolonging their stay in Rome, the two deputies asked and obtained permission to return to their monasteries. On February 21st, 1666, they solicited a final audience with the Holy Father who, as De Rancé never doubted, had been always sympathetic with the now lost cause. Alexander received them both with special marks of favour, but said not a word about the Reform. De Rancé next proceeded to take his leave of the Cardinal Protector of the Cistercian Order, the most determined opponent of the Strict Observance. He told the Cardinal with great candour what he thought of his conduct. And when his Eminence reminded him of the respect due to a prince of the Church, the Abbot replied : " I am speaking to you as St. Bernard spoke to the Sovereign Pontiffs of his own and after times, even much less strongly, and nevertheless they have never ceased to regard him as their most zealous defender and most firm support. The true friends of the Holy See are not those who know how to dissemble, but those rather who represent to it humbly all that concerns its glory." The Cardinal, speaking of the interview to a friend some time later, said : '' I cannot help admiring the presence of mind of this Abbot de Rancé and his extraordinary talent for telling the truth.''

On the day following their audience with the Pope a messenger arrived at their lodgings bearing three boxes, presents from the Holy Father. One box contained indulgenced medals, the two others were filled with sacred relics of great importance. It was Alexander's way of showing his good-will.

The two Abbots, very sad indeed, but fully resigned to the holy Will of God, left Rome for good on March 25th, the feast of the Annunciation.

CHAPTER XII.

*The Abbé Nicaise—The Pilgrim of Science with
the " Pilgrim of Eternity "—Visit to Clairvaux—
Austerities of La Trappe—Dearth of Vocations
—Extraordinary General Chapter—A Forged
Letter—Manner of Receiving Postulants —
François Cornuty—Regime at La Trappe —
Etienne le Camus.*

ON the return journey the deputies were accompanied as far as Florence by the Abbé Nicaise, one
who, though neither a great scientist nor a great
artist, was at least a great admirer of science and
art. He assiduously cultivated the acquaintance of
all the celebrities of his time, having plenty of money
and leisure. His meeting with De Rancé was therefore regarded by him as a very fortunate circumstance. " On my second journey from Rome to
France," he writes, " I travelled with the Abbot
of La Trappe. Judge if I were not well accompanied ! I had reason to congratulate myself on
this happy rencontre, and was able to derive much
profit therefrom, because from that time I have
kept up a correspondence with the holy Abbot,
which is to me a source of great consolation." De

Rancé had but little interest in the virtuoso's art or science or literary gossip, but very much in his soul. Nicaise professed to have a strong inclination for the religious life as practised by the Reformed Cistercians ; but whether he spoke sincerely or not, he never entered the cloister, and the Abbot of La Trappe wasted many letters and no end of spiritual advice on him.

As his way brought him near the abbey of Clairvaux, Abbot de Rancé turned aside to visit the tomb of St Bernard. On entering the poor hermitage called the Little St. Bernard, said to have been the first building erected by the Saint in the Valley of Wormwood, he threw himself prostrate on the ground, and remained thus until he was obliged to leave the place at nightfall. Next morning he asked permission of the Abbot, Dom Pierre-Henri, to spend the rest of his life as a recluse in that holy shrine. Like St. Peter on the Mount, he was beside himself with religious emotion and " knew not what he said." Abbot Henri, who showed him every kindness, regretted that he could not comply with a request so extraordinary.

The Abbot of La Trappe arrived at his monastery on May 10th, after an absence of twenty months. He found that his community had considerably increased in numbers. Three new novices of great promise had been received : the two brothers Duplessis de Grande Maison, belonging to one of the best families of Champagne, and the Abbé Alain Morony, formerly a professor of theology at St. Bernard's College, Paris, who had left the Common Observance in order to join the Reform at La Trappe. All three persevered in their holy vocation, all three came to be regarded as models even in that community of saints, and all three died in the odour of sanctity.

Now more than ever Abbot de Rancé's watch-word was : " Back to St. Bernard ! " No half reforms would satisfy him. He wanted to see the Holy Rule of St. Benedict observed at La Trappe as it had been observed during the first centuries of the Order's existence. He knew he could count on the co-operation of his own monks : his burning discourses had already inspired them with such an enthusiasm for penance that the difficulty was to keep them within bounds. But he did not know what attitude the Abbot of Citeaux, to whose jurisdiction he expected to be submitted very soon, would adopt with regard to his Reform. If it were not permitted him to follow the guidance of his conscience in this matter, there was nothing for it but to make use of his indult and pass over to La Grande Chartreuse.

The Abbot was always the first to practise what he desired to see practised by the community. He set the example and waited for the monks to ask permission to imitate him : like Our Blessed Lord

'' he began to do and to teach,'' the doing regularly anticipating the teaching. Thus, without any use of his authority, he had fish, eggs, and butter excluded from the refectory ; the recreation after dinner was restricted to three days in the week and during Lent to Sundays, the weekly long walks outside the enclosure went out of vogue, and several old-fashioned exercises of mortification, especially reprimands and penances in chapter, were restored to vigorous vitality.

The outside world heard with wonder of the austerities practised in Our Lady of La Trappe, and of course passed judgment on the Abbot. Some accused him of fanaticism, others of tyranny, all of foolish presumption. He did not mind their criticism much. What he did mind was the fact that no postulants were coming. This lack of vocations might be nothing more than a trial, such as Citeaux had to endure after its foundation, but it might also be reasonably interpreted as the judgment of God upon his undertaking. Besides he was in urgent need of additional subjects to carry on. He addressed himself to the Vicar-General, Abbot Jouaud of Prières, asking him to send some novices to La Trappe. The reply was not encouraging. '' You must be content with the religious you have,'' wrote Abbot Jouaud, '' and wait until it pleases God to send you novices animated with your own spirit. I don't think many such are to be found in other monasteries. And let me warn you that you will have more admirers than imitators of your Reform.'' It looked now as if La Trappe would be altogether isolated in the Order, disowned in a sense by both the Strict and the Common Observance. That certainly would sadden De Rancé, but it would not make him abandon his design. He was quite prepared to plough a lonely furrow. If he could not expect the sympathy of Abbot Jouaud or Abbot Vaussin, he could be sure of the blessing of SS. Benedict and Bernard.

In the autumn of 1666 a circular letter from the Abbot of Citeaux summoned all the other abbots of the Order, in virtue of holy obedience, to attend an extraordinary General Chapter which would open on May 9th of the following year. The purpose of the assembly was to publish the papal Brief deciding the controversy between the two Observances, which had at last arrived from Rome, and to pro-claim their loyalty to the Sovereign Pontiff by their humble acceptance of its provisions. Some of the abbots of the Strict Observance considered that they had better remain at home : why should they journey so far to witness their own defeat and the triumph of their opponents? However, wiser counsels prevailed. As Abbot de Rancé pointed out, their abstention from the General Chapter on this occasion would certainly be construed and represented as an act of insubordination to the pontifical authority.

The General Chapter opened on the day appointed, and was the most numerously attended that had been witnessed for many a year. After some preliminaries the Brief was read. It gave a death-blow to the aspirations of the Reformers. They lost their Vicar-General and their particular assemblies, and were put under the jurisdiction of the Abbot of Citeaux. Nothing could compensate in their eyes for this utter ruin of their hopes, yet they were not left altogether without consolation. They were allowed to follow their own Observance in their own houses, one-third of the definitors, that is, the officers who assisted the Abbot-General in the government of the Order, should be chosen from their number, and the Abbot-General himself was obliged, in virtue of holy obedience, to treat them with justice and charity, nay, to employ all his authority for the propagation of their Observance. When the secretary had finished reading the Brief, he handed it to the Abbot of Citeaux, who knelt to receive it and kissed it devoutly. Rising, he solemnly declared he would do all in his power to secure its exact observance by all those whom Divine Providence had placed under his charge. Several other abbots followed his example. Then the Abbot of La Trappe requested permission to speak. Having obtained his request, he said that, although aware that many clauses had been slipped into the Brief without the knowledge, and contrary to the will, of the Sovereign Pontiff, he, nevertheless, out of respect for the Holy See recommended its acceptance, until such time as the opportunity for an appeal for its revision should present itself.

The Chapter named the Abbot of La Trappe one of the ten definitors who were to represent the Strict Observance in the Abbot-General's council. The Abbot-General himself, desirous to show his esteem for an honourable opponent (to whom he was nearly related by consanguinity) asked him to undertake the office of canonical visitor for the provinces of Normandy, Brittany and Anjou. This was an important charge, and would give De Rancé a golden opportunity for propagating his ideas and protecting the interests of the Reform. But then it would mean so much distraction, so many excursions from his monastery. So he respectfully declined. His observations at the General Chapter with respect to the papal Brief were reported to the Holy See—viewed apart from their context and circumstances they appeared bold enough—with the result that in the Bull of confirmation issued by Clement IX, successor to Alexander VII, he was mentioned by name as one of the leaders of the opposition, and the appeal he had referred to refused in advance.

Amidst these afflictions, so manifold and multiform, he enjoyed the consolation of receiving into his monastery several good subjects. After all, God willed his work to endure. He had not, as was feared, cursed it with the curse of barrenness, but was rather blessing it with the choice blessing of fertility. And what matter about anything else when one's work has the blessing of God? But the increase in his numbers seems to have excited feelings of jealousy in certain quarters which manifested itself in a most dastardly attempt to injure La Trappe and its Abbot in the eyes of the public.

Most religious Orders then as always required a dowry from each postulant. There is a story of a zealous French preacher who announced that, after the sermon, a collection would be made for a young girl anxious to enter religion, but too poor to make a vow of poverty. Abbot de Rancé never asked a dowry, nevertheless a letter bearing his name was put in circulation which tended to produce the opposite impression. It was addressed to a prospective postulant and filled with the most disgusting haggling about the amount of money he was to bring. Numerous copies of this precious document were made, so that it fell into the hands of many. De Rancé knew about the forgery, but took no steps to expose it. In truth, there should have been no necessity, for commercialism would be about the last thing his acquaintances would think of reproaching him with. At last, however, he broke silence when the prior of St. Martin of Pontoise asked him to declare formally if he disowned the letter. " The letter in question," he replied, " is the work of a forger. It does not represent either my style or the maxims which I make the rule of my conduct. By the mercy of God, I have never yet exacted or desired a dowry from any of those whom Providence has conducted to La Trappe. All our receptions are gratuitous."

Yet, so far from being wealthy, the community of La Trappe had all they could do to make ends meet.

Amongst the postulants who presented themselves at this period, there were three deserving of special mention. François Cornuty, a youth belonging to the *haute noblesse* of Savoy, entered the Cistercian monastery of Tamié, in that country, and whilst still a novice was sent to St. Bernard's College,[1] Paris, to study his theology. Whilst there he heard of the wonderful reform that was being carried out at La Trappe and of the edifying lives of the monks. The news inspired him with enthusiasm whence emerged the resolve to apply

1 The college of St. Bernard, founded in 1250, by Stephen Lexington, Abbot of Clairvaux, was occupied by those young religious of the Cistercian Order who were studying for degrees at the Sorbonne. Both Observances patronised the institution, each maintaining there its own regime and its own horarium. At one time the Cistercians possessed similar colleges affiliated to more than forty of the great European universities.

for admission to that fervent community. In imitation of St. Stanislaus Kostka, he left the college secretly and travelled on foot to La Trappe. The journey took him six days to complete. As he had no money, he was obliged to beg his food on the way, and he slept wherever night overtook him. As soon as he came in sight of the monastery, falling on his knees, he cried out in the words of the Psalmist : '' How lovely are Thy tabernacles, O Lord God of hosts ! My soul longeth and fainteth for the courts of the Lord '' (Ps. lxxxiii, 1).

Another important recruit was Father Rigobert Lévêque, prior of the Cistercian house of Hautefontaine, of the Common Observance, who obtained permission from his superiors to enter the community of La Trappe.

Dom Eustache de Beaufort, Abbot of Septfons, one of the first filiations of Citeaux, situated in the province of Bourbonnais, had a history very similar to that of De Rancé. He, too, at an early age became a commendatory abbot, and squandered the revenues of his monastery in the gratification of his passions. His life gave so much scandal that the diocesan threatened to complain him to the King unless he made a retreat in a certain Franciscan convent. From that retreat he came forth a changed man. Like De Rancé, he took the Cistercian habit, and began to rule in Septfons as regular abbot. Hearing of La Trappe and its

fervent community, he went to request admission
there as a simple postulant. De Rancé, however,
refused to accept him. He told him to go back
and in his own monastery endeavour to restore the
full observance of St. Benedict's Rule. " By
remaining with us, you will only save your own
soul, but if you return to Septfons you will contribute
to the salvation of many."

Not alone Cistercians from other houses, but
also professed religious from other Orders presented themselves as postulants at La Trappe, and
with greater frequency according as the good odour
of Christ exhaling from that monastery began to
diffuse itself more and more widely. It was not
that Abbot de Rancé employed any kind of touting
to bring these subjects, or any kind of coaxing to
keep them. Much rather the contrary. The use
of human inducements in the matter of vocations
he would consider a sacrilege. To draw postulants
and to keep them he depended on the grace of
God alone. His own methods were more calculated
to deter them from coming, and to frighten them
away when they came. In answer to a letter of
application he wrote : " If you are determined to
abandon yourself unreservedly to Divine Providence ; if the roughness of our long winters, the
severity of the climate, the privation of all intercourse with men, the want of every human consolation for the rest of your life ; if all the consequences

of an entire self-renunciation do not trouble your heart ; if the love of God, and the desire to live exclusively for Him and to have no other occupation than that of awaiting His coming, if the thought of that eternity which is always nearer to us than we suppose—if these things make you regard as a moment the duration of your earthly existence, you may come.'' Rather discouraging. But then La Trappe was destined to be the home of heroes and none but heroic hearts had any business there.

When the aspirant, undismayed by the prospect placed before him, arrived at the monastery he received but a cold welcome. He had to remain several weeks on retreat in the guest-house, occupying his time in prayer, spiritual reading, and in the study of the Trappist life at close range. The Abbot and novice master visited him frequently to put vividly before his mind the privations and hardships he would have to endure at La Trappe. One would have imagined they were animated with an eager desire to see him abandoning his purpose. But their conduct was only such as St. Benedict's Rule prescribes : We have already quoted what the Saint enjoins with regard to the reception of postulants. They must first be subjected to humiliations and trials, and kept waiting outside the door for several days, uncertain as to whether they shall be accepted or rejected. If any has the fortitude to endure these trials with patience and humility, he may be admitted. But he must be told " all the difficulties and trials " of the life he is about to embrace.

When at last the postulant saw himself inside the noviciate, he found that he was only at the beginning of his troubles. Everything in the life at La Trappe was deliberately designed for the destruction of pride and sensuality. A man courageous enough to face the hungry lions and tigers of the amphitheatre might easily shrink from the sacrifices imposed on the Trappist monk. He rose from his hard bed in the morning never later than 2 a.m., on Sundays and feast days at 1 a.m., and on certain great festivals at midnight. On working days he divided his time between prayer and pious reading until the High Mass about 9 a.m., after which he went to work in the fields. From Easter to Holy Cross, September 14th, he broke his fast at noon and had supper in the evening. During the rest of the year he got nothing to eat until 2.30 p.m., and in Lent, 4.15 p.m.[2] And the food offered him required the seasoning of hunger to render it palatable—black bread and course vegetables with no condiment except salt. All the time his lips were sealed with the seal of perpetual silence : the hour's recreation

---

[2] After a trial of some years De Rancé found that, in spite of their goodwill, his religious were unable to endure a fast of such severity. Thereupon he decided to have dinner never later than noon. But the more rigorous regime was resumed by his successors.

was a thing of the past. The more worldly advantages
possessed by the novice the more mercilessly he
was humbled. Abbot de Rancé made that his settled
policy. He appointed to the two meanest offices
in the monastery a gentleman of distinguished birth
and education, and a military officer of high rank.

Fervent novices ran no risk of having their heads
turned with ill-advised praise at Our Lady of La
Trappe. Young Cornuty gave every sign of eminent
sanctity during his noviciate. One morning he
accused himself in chapter, according to Cistercian
custom, of a slight fault of inadvertance against the
Rule. The Abbot reproved him with terrible
severity and ordered him to take the discipline.
Then he said : '' It is only out of compassion and
charity we have put up with you so long. But now
it becomes necessary to drive away the diseased
sheep lest it should infect the whole flock. Leave
the chapter, for you are unworthy to associate with
the religious of La Trappe.'' When the poor
novice, broken-hearted, had gone to seek consolation before the Tabernacle, the Abbot said to the
community : '' You know, my dear brethren, the
piety and regularity of this novice. For my part
I regard him as a vessel of election, as a present
which heaven has made to La Trappe. It is not
merely for our edification, but for our humiliation
and confusion that God has sent him amongst us.
In treating him as I have done, I have had nothing

else in view but to give you proof of the genuineness
of his vocation, and to make known to you how
firmly established he is in virtue. Pray that God
may continue to shower His favours upon him and
give him the grace of perseverance."

On a certain occasion one of the novices committed a fault against discipline. Not knowing who
the culprit was, the Abbot in chapter asked him to
declare himself. Nobody moved. Then the Abbot
rose from his seat, and in a voice that made everybody in the room tremble, said : " My brethren,
what have we come to ? The fault against discipline
is of no consequence, but this dissimulation is a
matter so serious in a community where one makes
profession to serve God perfectly, that I cannot
permit novices of such dispositions to take the
monastic vows. I pray God that my right arm
may wither before I receive into the community of
La Trappe any persons who, after committing a
fault, have not the humility to confess it. I am
half-minded to dismiss all the novices in order to
avoid the danger of admitting this coward." That
brought the culprit to the light. Throwing himself
at the Abbot's feet he humbly begged forgiveness.
He obtained it easily. But to expiate his fault of
dissimulation the whole communty had to fast for
one day on bread and water.

The summer of 1667 brought Abbot de Rancé
a very sweet consolation. Of his friends of former

days there was none dearer to him than Etienne le Camus. Many the escapade and adventure they shared together in the thoughtless times of youth. But when De Rancé was touched by grace and turned to God, his friend remained entangled in the world. Honours and wealth rendered life very smooth for him : already he had attained to the important office of almoner to the King, which was but one remove from a bishopric. Hearing about the extra-ordinary life his whilom friend was leading, he thought he would " go and see this strange sight." So he spent some days as the guest of De Rancé. When he returned to Paris there was little of the old pleasure-loving Le Camus to be found in him. He immediately renounced his benefices with a yearly revenue of 40,000 francs, and would have resigned his office of royal almoner but the King refused to accept his resignation. He declined the bishopric of Bazas, offered him by Louis XIV. And he never tired talking about De Rancé and his monks. At the King's request he gave the court a detailed account of his experiences at La Trappe, where were being renewed the wonders of the Thebaid. We shall meet Le Camus again.

CHAPTER XIII.

Trouble with the Celestins—De Retz amongst the
Prophets—Trouble with the Strict Observance
—De Rancé co-operates in the Reform of
Convents.

IN 1667 a professed monk of the Order of Celestins
applied for admission at La Trappe and, as he
seemed to possess the necessary qualifications,
was received. His former superiors felt much
aggrieved at his conduct in leaving them and not less
so at the conduct of De Rancé in accepting him.
They went so far as to declare both Puiperron—
the monk's name—and the Abbot of La Trappe
excommunicated. The Provincial of the Celestins
made a formal demand for the return of his subject.
De Rancé had no difficulty in showing that neither
he nor Puiperron had in anything overstepped the
limits of his rights. His answer put an end to the
controversy, but only for the time being. After
the Celestin came a Canon Regular of Paris, Pierre
le Nain, son of the Master of Appeals, and brother
to the illustrious historian, Sebastian le Nain de
Tillemont. It was Pierre's destiny, after being
closely associated with De Rancé during the next

thirty-three years, to bequeath to posterity a living portrait of his beloved master.

At the beginning of the year 1668 the Abbot of La Trappe received a letter that surprised him a good deal, and embarrassed him not a little. The letter came from Cardinal de Retz, and it was nothing less than an application for admission to La Trappe. We have said the application embarrassed De Rancé, because although the Abbot admired his Eminence as a scholar and as a statesman he did not think he had in him the makings of a monk. However, he visited the Cardinal at the latter's urgent request (De Retz was then living retired at his château in Commercy) in order to talk matters over He told him plainly that the Trappist regime would suit neither his health nor his disposition, and recommended him, if, as he professed, he desired to give himself to God in religion, to enter a less severe Order. The Cardinal felt disappointed, yet did not die of a broken heart. He promised the Abbot that he would turn over a new leaf and begin a life of fervour and of exclusive preoccupation with the things of eternity. After waiting in vain a considerable time for the fulfilment of this promise, De Rancé sent him a letter which testifies to the fearless candour of him who wrote it, but not less to the humility of him who received it :—

" I conjure your Eminence, in the name of God, to recall to mind what you had the goodness to

communicate to me the last time I had the honour
to meet you at Commercy. Several years have
gone by since then, and it appears to me the project on which you were so bent on that occasion
has not been advanced very much. Yet time and
all things temporal are speeding away from us with
most terrifying velocity, and God's eternity is
drawing near—that ocean, limitless in expanse,
fathomless in depth, wherein the lives of mortals,
even the most renowned and illustrious, must lose
themselves and be confounded. I am sure your
Eminence will not take offence at my boldness.
You know that it springs from affection, and that
my words only express the anxiety of my heart.''

This letter made a deep impression on De Retz.
If he did not enter the cloister he at least began
to live in a way less unworthy of an ecclesiastic.
He actually wished to renounce his dignity as
cardinal, but Pope Clement X would not permit
him. And from that time until his death in 1679 the
beacon-light of La Trappe continued to guide his
footsteps heavenward.

About the same time (Spring, 1668) Dom
Charles Henri de Benzeradt, Abbot of the Cistercian
monastery of Orval in the diocese of Frier, Luxem-
burg, announced his intention of introducing the
Trappist reform into his own community. He came
to consult De Rancé about the matter. When he
saw how the monks of La Trappe lived he lost

courage and exclaimed : " Do you forget, Father
Abbot, that these religious of yours are but men,
living in the same mortal bodies as you and I, and
not impassible spirits?" However, he persevered
in his purpose, and with the help of monks lent
him from La Trappe succeeded in making his house
a model of regularity. From Orval the reform
extended to the monasteries of Dulceldad in
Germany and Beaupré in Lorraine.

Not long after his interview with the Abbot of
Orval, De Rancé was requested by Dom le Roy,
commendatory Abbot of Hautefontaine, diocese of
Châlons-sur-Marne, to co-operate in the reform of
that monastery, and to permit Father Rigobert,
one of his religious, and formerly prior of the
monastery in question, to return thither as regular
abbot. Having consulted Father Rigobert on the
subject, he declared the proposal quite impracticable This brought a fresh storm about his ears.
The superiors of the Strict Observance denounced
him as a traitor to the cause ; the Abbot of Prières,
formerly Vicar-General, wrote to say he was
scandalised at his refusal to extend the kingdom of
God. Nothing could be gentler or more humble
than his reply to this harsh reproof from one who
was no longer his superior :—

" My very Rev. Father, so long as I live I
shall receive with all due respect all the instructions
which you will have the goodness to give me. I

regret extremely that the sentiments shared by Father Rigobert and myself should have appeared to you so extraordinary and unchristian as to scandalise you to the degree your letter proclaims. That of itself should more than suffice to make you see how unworthy both of us are to have the direction of souls. He is fortunate to have escaped that charge. As for myself, if God opened for me a way out of the pastoral office as unmistakably as He has blocked the way into that office against Father Rigobert, I assure your Reverence I would not remain one moment longer in the place where I am. It is impossible for me to change my opinion with regard to this matter. If Father Rigobert and I are making a mistake, he in refusing the office and I in not venturing to counsel his acceptance, I trust that Our Lord Jesus Christ, Who knows the dispositions of our hearts, will mercifully pardon the sin of our ignorance, and will not judge it in His severity.''

It will be remembered that two of Abbot de Rancé's sisters, Frances and Marie-Louise, entered the convent of the Annonciades in Paris. Both persevered in their vocation and became exemplary religieuses. Needless to say, this house possessed quite a particular interest for the Abbot of La Trappe. The rule observed by the Annonciades (their full title was Annonciades Celestials) was very strict, and required a complete separation from the world.[1] This proved—or seemed to prove—a hindrance to vocations so that the community dwindled. Several of the nuns joined in the demand from outside for some modification of the law of enclosure ; otherwise, they said, the convent would soon be untenanted. The superioress, a good, pious soul, did not know what to do. She consulted the Abbot of La Trappe, and was answered in a letter worthy of St. Bernard :

" Remember your obligations. Remember that you have promised God by a solemn vow to maintain the grilles and the enclosure in the manner in which they have been established from the beginning. I do not see how you can dispense yourself from an obligation so pressing, how you can conscientiously disengage yourself from a contract made at the foot of the altar. The conservation of your convent must never engross your solicitude to the prejudice of what you owe to God. He does not will that we should do what is good, howsoever great that good may appear to our eyes, by ways which are not permitted us ; and it is an evident sign that He does not exact the good of us when He leaves us no legitimate way of accomplishing it. If the whole universe was on the point of perishing, I should be bound, in order to prevent

[1] The nuns of this Order made a fourth vow to open the grille only three times a year to see their parents, brothers and sisters, and never directly or indirectly to take any step towards procuring a modification of this same vow.

the ruin, to take no single step that would not be according to the Divine Will and ordinance. Such is the sentiment of the saints. And can you imagine that you are acting according to the Will of God in violating a law so holy? Or that your conduct is in harmony with His ordinance when you fail to keep the important and public pledge you have given Him? Though your Institute should be annihilated and you could only have saved it by unlawful means, its destruction would not be imputed to you. But, on the other hand, if you are wanting to the vow you have made to God, be sure He will hold you to account for that, and He will judge your infidelity according to the rigour of His justice.

"What! God wills for your particular preservation, that you should have but very little commerce with the world, and you believe you cannot be preserved without much greater commerce than He has authorised! God has closed your gates and your grilles to the end that you may persevere in the fidelity and purity which you owe Him, and you pretend that, in order to maintain yourselves, it is necessary to open those same gates and grilles! Believe me, it is difficult to reach the same goal by ways so divergent, so contrary. Of necessity, either He is deceived or you are deceived. Remember, finally, that nowadays there is much more reason than ever before for separating yourselves from the world, the corruption of society being incomparably more dangerous, and the weakness of human nature being far greater now than at the time of your institution.''

The Abbot's weighty words impressed the mother-superioress, and the grilles were kept closed as he counselled. Henceforth as heretofore, the poor nuns should be content with seeing their own side of the enclosure wall.

In 1670 the Abbot's authority was invoked to settle the affairs of another convent, the Cistercian convent of Saint-Antoine, the same in which his father's sister, Marie, had been abbess until her death in 1652. The most fervent of the nuns, although in a minority, desired to follow the Strict Observance, even considered themselves bound thereto, since Pope Alexander in his Brief had expressed the wish to see all the members of the Cistercian Order walking in the footsteps of their holy founders. But their superiors forbade them to make any change. In their distress they appealed to the Abbot of La Trappe. He encouraged them to persevere in their demands : they were acting in accordance with the desire and intention of the Sovereign Pontiff, Christ's Vicar on earth, and so were justified in their resistance to inferior authority ; if there be a silence and a passivity that belong to virtue, there may also be the silence and passivity that result from death. Somebody wrote a public letter against De Rancé, accusing him of fomenting discord in the convent, and sacrificing union and charity to the interests of asceticism. The Abbot had not much trouble in refuting his critic. Union, obviously, is not always a good nor is singularity always an evil ; and so far from encouraging the nuns to resist authority, he rather encouraged them to resist the resisters of authority. This struggle endured for three and a half years, and ended in the complete triumph of the reforming party.

Victor le Bouthillier, Archbishop of Tours, died on September 12th, 1670, after two days' illness. When the news reached his nephew, the Abbot of La Trappe, he exclaimed : " My God ! Only two days to settle his accounts after forty years in the episcopate ! It is terrible." The Archbishop had but little in common with his illustrious predecessor, St. Martin ; still he was a good man and rendered important services to religion. To him the archdiocese owed the establishment of the Capuchins and the nuns of the Visitation.

In the same year died Claude Vaussin, Abbot of Citeaux, and Superior-General of the Cistercian Order. He was succeeded by Jean Petit. This event greatly rejoiced the Abbot of La Trappe, for Dom Petit was known to be in sympathy with the Reform. He wrote to congratulate the new General on his election, and to express the hope that his administration would mark a second golden epoch in the history of the Institute whose honour they had both so much at heart.

Another important incident of this year was an application made to Abbot de Rancé by Mgr. de Caulet, the pious Bishop of Pamiers, for a colony of his monks to found a new monastery under the shadow of the Pyrenees. The Abbot very willingly promised to grant the request, he even resolved to retire himself to this new foundation where he would have more solitude and more time for prayer than he enjoyed at La Trappe. " My determination is," he wrote to the Bishop, " to withdraw for the rest of my life to the projected establishment, so as to finish under your protection the course of penance I have so badly begun. I am assured that, when I tell you my reasons for desiring to separate myself still more from my acquaintances and to bury myself more completely than I have done, you will not disapprove." However, the project of the new foundation came to nothing. King Louis XIV forbade the erection of any more religious establishments without his formal permission, which, it appears, Mgr. de Caulet was not able to obtain.

CHAPTER XIV.

*Revival of the controversy with the Celestins—
Publication of the Constitutions of La Trappe—
Controversy with Le Roy—Marshal Bellefonds—
Spread of Reform—Madame de la Valliere—
Death Scenes—Renewal of Vows.*

WE have spoken of a controversy between the
Abbot of La Trappe and the Celestin superiors,
occasioned by his reception of one of their subjects.
It revived in 1670 when seven other members of
the same Order applied for admission to La Trappe
and were received. There was a tremendous outcry.
De Rancé became a target for all kinds of abuse
and denunciation. Here is how he answered his
critics : the letter is addressed to the Provincial of
the Celestins :—

" I have never solicited any of your subjects to
leave the Order in which they made profession ; I
have never done anything, directly or indirectly, to
draw any of them to La Trappe. But, Reverend
Father, let me tell you this : a very long time ago
the majority of those who have now come to us
wrote to me of their dispositions and acquainted me
with the desires of their heart, and I refused to

reply to their letters. However, God's hour having arrived, they came to seek us, and His finger was so plainly visible in the execution of their design and in all the circumstances preceding it, that in truth, Reverend Father, I could not conscientiously reject the souls that seemed to have been conducted to me by the hand of the Lord Himself. ' Who was I that could withstand God?' (Acts xi., 17). I desired with all my heart that you would permit them to enjoy in peace the liberty which God has given them, and which the Church has preserved to them, so that they might not be constrained to publish their reasons for leaving you. God knows, Reverend Father, how grieved I am at the condition to which you declare you have been reduced by their departure, and that I would do all in my power for your consolation and the re-establishment of discipline in your Order. Nevertheless, being persuaded that I have received these religious from the hand of God, and that He has given me charge of their souls, I cannot do otherwise than keep them, so far as it lies in my power, in order to be able to render an account of them when He shall demand it at the judgment to which you in your letter cite me, and before which very soon both you and I must appear. . . . . However provoking the letters you send me, I will never answer you otherwise than as Christian charity dictates.''

The Provincial offered a compromise : he would

consent to De Rancé's retaining the seven on
condition that he promised to receive no more
Celestins. This proposal the Abbot could not accept,
and for the same reasons that determined him to
receive the monks in question : it would be an
invasion of God-given rights and a hindrance to the
action of His Spirit. However, he submitted the
case to the theological faculty of the Sorbonne.
Their decision appeared on July 3rd, 1671. The
doctors were unanimous in favour of De Rancé,
and condemned the Provincial's proposal as unjust.
But when yet another Celestin entered La Trappe,
and the Superior-General complained that the loss
of his best subjects left him powerless to effect a
contemplated reform of his Institute, the Abbot
promised to admit no more applicants from that
Order.

The most important event of the year 1671 was
the publication of the Constitutions of Our Lady of
La Trappe. De Rancé himself had nothing to do
with it. A visitor at the monastery got hold of the
manuscript used for the guidance of the monks,
and without the authorisation or knowledge of the
Abbot had it printed and published in Paris.

The same year the grand vicar of Aleth entered
the noviciate. By this time the community had increased so much that the monastery required to be
enlarged. Thirty-four new cells were erected. But
this would only relieve the congestion temporarily, as

the postulants kept coming in ever greater numbers. Yet something happened just then that was well calculated to put a period to the prosperity of La Trappe. The Abbé le Roy paid a visit to the monastery and at his own urgent request was permitted to take part in all the community exercises. Far from being edified, he was shocked and scandalised at many things he witnessed, particularly at the way in which the Abbot publicly humiliated the monks. Nor did he make any secret of his impressions. He even warned De Rancé of his intention to publish a critique of the Trappist asceticism. The critique appeared in due course. Its chief object of attack was the Abbot's practice of imposing penances where there appeared no moral fault. Such a practice was opposed to the gentleness of Jesus Christ, to Christian charity, which obliges us to put a favourable construction on the actions of our neighbour, even to truth, since one pretended to see faults where none existed —it was a piece of *foulerie spirituelle*, yet dangerous too.

De Rancé required a good deal of urging to answer his critic. When he did so it was to some purpose. Le Roy viewed monastic penances from a completely wrong standpoint. Were they intended as purely vindictive punishments, his condemnation would be just. But such was not the case. These penances served three objects : they served to expiate any fault there might be, to atone for the past, and to preserve humility. There was no question of formal guilt, but only of material transgressions of disciplinary rules. To deny the right of imposing penances for such would amount to an indictment of all religious institutes, indeed of all human governments, ecclesiastical and civil. Le Roy, urged on by his Jansenist associates, attempted a reply ; but this time he was answered by Bossuet. It was an unequal contest : the mouse against the lion and the eagle. Le Roy had no more to say.[1]

There was another distinguished visitor at La Trappe about the same time as Le Roy, but of a very different disposition. This was M. Pellison, the illustrious statesman and scholar, as yet a Protestant. According to Le Nain, '' he was so impressed by the virtuous conduct of the incarnate angels whom he saw there, that he renounced his heresy, and lived thenceforward as a perfect Christian.''

Amongst De Rance's military friends—and they were many—the most distinguished was Marshal Bellefonds. This gallant and gifted officer, having refused to take orders from Turenne in 1672, saw

---

[1] The author of the *Abbé Tempête* repeats Le Roy's shallow criticism. He has gathered together so many yarns illustrative of De Rancé's severity that one wonders how he overlooked the case of the novice who was dismissed because his uproarious slumbers at the time of meditation used to awaken the Abbot !

himself degraded by the Sovereign. Of the numerous friends he counted in the days of his glory, only two had the courage to stand by him in his disgrace—Bossuet, now Bishop of Meaux, and De Rancé. The latter, as soon as he heard of his misfortune, wrote to console him in these terms : " The saints, who were filled with the spirit of truth, considered such high positions as that from which Providence has withdrawn you to be an almost insurmountable obstacle to salvation. They went so far as to say that posts of the kind rendered salvation morally impossible. Consequently, if we look at things, as they did, with the eyes of faith, we ought in your behalf to thank God for having in a moment destroyed so many impediments to your eternal happiness and provided you with so many means of sanctification. Everything here below passes with lightning speed, and there is nothing worthy to occupy a place in the heart of a Christian save God alone Who alone is eternal." The Marshal spent some time in retirement at La Trappe. After enduring his disgrace with Christian fortitude for several years, he was recalled to the army and restored to favour with the King. Later on, by De Rancé's advice, he entered La Grande Chartreuse.

Meantime, the fame of La Trappe and its fervent community was spreading in all directions and everywhere causing a searching of hearts. The splendid success of De Rancé's reform inspired other superiors with the courage to follow his example. With his counsel and zealous co-operation reforms similar to his own were effected in the monasteries of Du Pin, diocese of Poitiers, Champagne, diocese of Mans, Chaloché, diocese of Angers, and in the convent of Leime, diocese of Cahors. His letter to the holy Abbess of this convent, Mother de la Vieuville, powerfully sustained her reforming efforts in the face of the most determined opposition coming from a quarter whence encouragement might more reasonably be expected. He also co-operated with the Abbess Hollandine of Manubuisson in her successful endeavours to reform that convent.

We have not space for more than a passing reference to the eloquent memorial in behalf of the Strict Observance which he composed and presented to King Louis XIV in 1673. Bossuet might have equalled but could scarcely have surpassed it. But there is another incident much more to his credit which must not be omitted. He learned that the royal protection for the Strict Observance, which he had solicited and doubted if he would obtain, could be infallibly secured through the intermediacy of an unworthy woman ; moreover, that her intercession could be had for the asking. Anything in reason he would have done to promote the Reform ; suffering would be sweet if endured for its triumph. But he could not and would not sacrifice either his

honour or his conscience for any thing in the world.
He composed another Memoir which was presented
to a commission appointed by the King to inquire
into the grievances alleged by the Reformers.   It
was published under the title : *Eclaircissements sur
l'état présent de l'Ordre de Citeaux*. We may say
here that this commission disappointed the hopes
he had entertained of it, and left the Strict Observance in a worse condition than it was before.

It was a little before this time the Abbot of La
Trappe became acquainted with Madame de la
Vallière, whose life hitherto had been a public scandal. She owed her conversion principally to Bossuet,
but De Rancé, to whom she turned for counsel, confirmed her in the resolution she had taken to repair
the past by leading thenceforth a life of penance.
" I cannot prevent myself," she wrote to her friend,
Marshal Bellefonds, " from giving you a participation in the delight I experienced at seeing the
Abbot of La Trappe and receiving from his lips such
instructions as he imparts to his novices. He
exhorted me to preserve myself always in confidence
and peace of soul. Oh, how ardent is his love of
God in comparison with mine, and how this con-
founds me !   Am I not bound to love God more
than everybody else, considering all He has done
for me ?"   This poor penitent ended her days
happily in a Carmelite convent.

The penitential life led by the monks of La Trappe had at least this temporal reward that it robbed death of its terrors. Nothing can be more touching than the account preserved to us of some of these hallowed death-scenes. The religious breathed their last lying on a bed of ashes. Father Paul Hardy, formerly theologian to the Bishop of Aleth, suffered from a gangrened arm, and was asked by the Abbot to submit to a very painful operation. "Reverend Father," he answered smilingly, "this arm is no longer mine, it belongs to you." He died after the ordeal the death of the predestinate. "Reverend Father," whispered Father Charles with his dying breath, "I am going to Our Lord full of gladness and consolation." "I am going to God with perfect confidence and joy," were the parting words of Father Muce, "He has made use of you, Reverend Father, to save me. I owe my salvation to your charity." "I no longer hope," cried the expiring Father Bernard, "I have assurance." Brother Benedict, being asked if he were resigned to die, exclaimed: "Resigned! why I regard the day of my death as a feast day, like Christmas." Then thanking the Abbot for his kindness, he begged him to remain at his side, saying: "Reverend Father, you must excuse my presumption, but the only consolation I enjoy in this world is to see your face." The Abbot stood sentinel at every death-bed like a visible guardian

angel, praying for the final perseverance of the
sufferer the while he whispered words of comfort in
his ear. " Behold how he loved him !" the monks
could repeat. as one after another of their number
lay down to die. And how they loved him in return !
" From the first day to the last they were passion-
ately devoted to him," admits Bremond in one of
the few honest passages in his book, " they
practically adored him, forgave him everything—
or rather did not know there was anything to for-
give." Neither did their successors ever acquire
that knowledge. It was reserved for M. Bremond
to discover that Abbot de Rancé was a tyrant and
a hypocrite.

During the first half of the year 1675, the
community lost by death six or seven of its members,
several others were seriously ill, and all looked pale
and emaciated. The Abbot called the religious together, and after speaking of the mortality and
the general decline in health, asked if they desired
to abandon the severe fasts prescribed by the Holy
Rule as beyond their strength, or if, paying no
heed to the suggestions of human prudence, they
were resolved to persevere in the course they had
begun, and to put their trust in Providence. All,
without exception, declared for the retention of the
fasts. He then announced that he would ask all the
professed religious to renew their vows publicly on
June 26th of that year. It was truly an impressive

sight to see those monks, worn out with fasting and watching and ceaseless toil, standing in line before their Abbot and protesting before heaven and earth their invincible purpose to remain attached to the Cross of Christ until death came to deliver them.

CHAPTER XV.

Canonical Visitation of La Trappe—Abbot de Saumon—Du Suel—Dom Minguet—Publication of the " Relations " and its Result—Illness—Petition to the Pope—Answer of Innocent—De Rancé's Activity—Lectures in Chapter—Bishops advise a Modification of Trappist Austerity—The Abbot's Answer.

THREE times the Abbot of La Trappe had the honour of being asked to discharge the office of canonical visitor in the provinces of Brittany, Normandy and Anjou, and three times he felt obliged to excuse himself. The office was then given to Dom Hervé du Tertre, the new Abbot of Prières. Towards the end of 1676 this worthy prelate arrived at La Trappe to make his first visitation there. He came with strong prejudices against the Abbot, and with the conviction that he would have a very painful duty to perform. People had told him that Abbot de Rancé was hard and haughty, devoid of prudence and compassion, who treated his religious as slaves and loaded them with mortifications and penances beyond human strength to bear. He would put a stop to all that.

He had a private interview with every religious in the house without a single exception. They were assured of what they already knew : that every word they said to him would be kept an inviolable secret. And then they were asked to give their opinion of the superior. One after another, from the oldest to the youngest, they testified to their unbounded love and veneration for the Abbot. They could not find words sufficient to express their gratitude for his unwearying kindness and gentleness, and for his constant attention to their needs. The visitor could hardly believe his ears, but he could not doubt the evidence. The situation was somewhat embarrassing ; he had come hither prepared to do battle against a lion and lo ! he found himself confronted with a lamb. What follows is his official report of the visitation : —

" Having come to the abbey of La Trappe in our capacity as visitor of the monasteries of the Strict Observance in the provinces of Brittany, Normandy, Anjou, and adjacent districts, we found there the Reverend Father Armand-Jean as titular Abbot and with him thirty-three choir religious (of whom sixteen are priests, eleven clerics, and six novices) and twelve lay brothers, in all forty-six persons. We learned that they belong for the most part to different provinces, Anjou, Brittany, Normandy, Poitou, Burgundy, etc., that some have been students in different colleges, some cavaliers, some soldiers, some clerics, some doctors in theology ; others have passed hither from various Orders and Observances, as from the Canons-Regular, the Hermits of St. Augustine, the Benedictines, the Congregation of St. Maur, the Celestins, the Cordeliers, and even from other Cistercian houses both of the Common and the Strict Observance. Despite the great differences of country and condition, we have found them so closely united in the bonds of fraternal charity, so uniform in all things, so consistently zealous in the discharge of their duties, so universally solicitous to maintain regular observance, and enjoying a peace so profound, that during a secret scrutiny, which lasted three whole days, we heard not a single word of complaint from inferiors against superiors, or from superiors against inferiors. And not only have we discovered or remarked no discontent, murmuring, disunion, coldness, partiality, aversion or dislike amongst the religious, but not even the least appearance or shadow of such things. For all which both they and ourselves ought to render fervent and unceasing thanks to God. So we have not considered it necessary to make any new rules or ordinances, but merely to exhort them to strive to advance always to higher perfection by the practice of the penitential regime which they have embraced. And to the end that they may continue firm and unshaken in the perfect union and concord

wherewith God has hitherto blessed them, we have
conjured them ' by the bowels of the mercy of our
God,' Who has thus deigned to visit them with His
extraordinary graces, to persevere in the love and
practice of the means which His goodness has
placed at their disposal.''

The Abbot of Tamié, Jean-Antoine de la Forest
de Saumon, was considered the most zealous and
powerful opponent of the Reform. His great gifts
as well as his influence with the ruling classes made
him truly formidable. But if he disliked the general
Reform, as he undoubtedly did, he may be said to
have held the reform of La Trappe in abhorrence.
He could not endure to hear the name of that
monastery mentioned. Needless to say, Abbot de
Rancé had no more of his love than Christian
charity required. The reason of this special anti-
pathy to La Trappe and its superior was the
admission there of his most promising subject,
François Cornuty. De Saumon had moved heaven
and earth to compel the return of this religious,
but all in vain. He was on his way home from Paris
in September, 1677, when he felt an irresistible
impulse to visit the place for which he had so strong
an aversion, and to see for himself the fanatical
austerities of its inmates. *Venit, vidit, victus est* :
he came, he saw, he was conquered. The Abbot's
unaffected humility and gentle charity towards one
who had been his most determined opponent took

the visitor completely by surprise. His prejudices vanished. '' He admired the austerities which he saw practised, the silence so exactly observed, the gravity with which the Divine Office was chanted, the modest and respectful demeanour of the monks during this holy exercise, their assiduity at manual labour, above all, the serenity and joy depicted on their countenance.'' He passed the whole night in tears. Next morning he went and, prostrating himself at De Rancé's feet, humbly begged forgiveness for all he had done and said against himself and his community. Before leaving La Trappe he made a vow to introduce the Reform into his own abbey without loss of time. The Abbot of La Trappe sent four of his religious to assist him in that difficult undertaking. Thus François Cornuty returned as a reformer to the monastery which he had entered as a novice and expected never to see again.

Well-intentioned people were constantly getting the Abbot of La Trappe into trouble. Enthusiastic admiration may be all very fine, but it has its disadvantages, especially when the malignant sisters, Envy and Jealousy, are stalking abroad. The Abbé du Suel, doctor in theology, and curé of Chartres, came to La Trappe to join the community. Abbot de Rancé refused to admit him, believing he had no vocation—he was always very slow to receive curés. Du Suel then asked the favour of getting the Abbot's views on some monastic virtues and practices. This request he obtained. The matters discussed concerned silence, solitude, manual labour, etc. After each conference the visitor hurried off to his room in the guest quarters and put on paper all he could remember of De Rancé's discourse, supplying from his own imagination all he couldn't. Some time after his departure an anonymous book appeared, entitled : *Entretiens de l'abbé Jean et du prêtre Eusèbe*. Of course, everybody knew who l'abbé Jean was. The book had a great vogue. People compared it to the conferences of Cassian. But there were those who found fault with it, and with its reputed author, Abbot de Rancé. Not being brazen enough to publish his own praises over his own signature, they said, he had published the book anonymously. As a matter of fact the composition was two parts Du Suel to one part De Rancé, and the Abbot was as much surprised as annoyed when he heard of the publication.

Another abbot visited La Trappe at this time, not as De Saumon to study the life of the community, but to live that life. This was Dom Jacques Minguet, the saintly superior of the abbey of Châtillon, diocese of Verdun. He had passed his seventy-seventh birthday, when he presented himself for admission to the novitiate, putting himself in the hands of De Rancé " to be moulded to whatsoever form and figure he might please." He looked for and received no exemptions or privileges of any kind, and became a perfect model of every monastic virtue. The year after his profession he lost his sight, which so far from depressing him only added to his happiness. When dying two years later, he insisted on going to the church to receive the Holy Viaticum. To the astonishment of the attendants, he not only walked there without assistance, but knelt during the whole time of Mass. Returning after thanksgiving, he fell down and died at the entrance of his cell.

We shall mention another incident which, if not so edifying, has yet an interest of its own. A Cordelier came to La Trappe with the intention of joining the community. As he seemed to have all the necessary qualifications the Abbot accepted him. But at the last moment he lost heart : he would wait a little longer, he said ; he was still young, only thirty, and after a few years he would come back to stay. De Rancé represented to him the folly of counting upon the uncertain future. He only laughed at his fears : he felt in the pink of health. A few hours later he died suddenly in the guest quarters.

Aware of the importance of good example, and following the precedent of the ancient fathers, De Rancé wrote an account of the holy deaths he had witnessed in his monastery, to glorify after their departure those whom he had kept humble during life, and to encourage those who succeeded them to walk faithfully in their footsteps. He had no thought of publication. But Providence so arranged that the manuscript fell into the hands of an outsider who made no scruple about getting it printed. The book appeared under the title : *Relations de la mort de quelque religieux de la Trappe*. It aroused another furore. The Abbot of La Trappe was blowing his own horn, he was shamelessly boasting of the superiority of his religious over all others, he represented them as saints, so as to enhance his own credit. " God be praised in all things," he wrote to a sympathetic correspondent. " My comfort is that I have had no part in this publication. I wrote the *Relations* solely for the use of my brethren, not at all with a view to the public. This should be evident enough from the simplicity of the style. But I can assure you that all these storms do not in the least trouble me. It would be ridiculous for the last and most miserable of the servants to expect to be treated better than the Master. He who reflects on the terrible judgment of God has little to fear from human judges. My time is now so short that I should be a fool to waste any of it answering the criticisms of men. God has given us peace, He preserves us in peace, and do what they may men cannot deprive us thereof. His holy Will is all I desire, and His

Will shall be accomplished in spite of the whole world."

When the Abbot penned that letter he believed his death was at hand. His health had been on the decline for many years past. In 1672 he took ill on his way to the General Chapter, and was obliged to return to his monastery. From that time forward he hardly ever enjoyed a respite from physical suffering. His condition became so serious in 1677 that death was thought to be imminent. Nevertheless he kept up his practices of mortification : " I must continue to serve Jesus Christ," he said, " and die arms in hand."

Believing that after his death the monastery would again become the property—we had almost said the prey—of a commendatory abbot, he petitioned Pope Innocent XI for a Brief granting the community the right to elect a prior who should continue to govern them according to the Rule of St. Benedict and the traditions of the Cistercian Order ; this prior should hold office for three years, but might be re-elected, and should have practically the same powers as an abbot. The petition was accompanied with a personal and very intimate letter to His Holiness, wherein the Abbot tells of his conversion, of his retirement to La Trappe, of the zeal and fervour of his community, and of his absolute submission to the authority of the Apostolic See. Finally, he begged the Holy Father to give his protection and support to those who were striving for the complete reform of the Cistercian Institute. The Pope granted his petition with regard to the prior, and promised to take La Trappe under his special protection. " His Holiness," wrote Cardinal Cibo, Secretary of State, " accords you the favours you have petitioned and the most effectual succours to preserve and develop the discipline you have established. He adds this also, as you will see in the Brief, that he hopes in the Lord, Who has chosen you before all ages to be the author of so great a work, that those sublime practices of virtue and abstinence will tend to the edification and the spiritual advantage, not only of your Order, but of the whole French people, and to the glory of our age." " I can assure you," wrote another member of the papal court, " that His Holiness so strongly approves of the apostolic manner of life which you have established in La Trappe that he will embrace every opportunity which offers to second your efforts and to preserve the fruits thereof to posterity."[1]

These testimonies of approbation and goodwill from the highest authority on earth rejoiced the heart of the holy Abbot, and more than made amends

[1] Thus the Order through its visitor approved of De Rancé's government, and the Church through her Pontiff. The Abbot might perhaps consider himself secure now? Alas, no. For he has still to reckon with M. Henri Bremond.

for all the calumnies of which he was the object. They were the more welcome inasmuch as he had been informed by Cardinal Bona that there were people in Rome endeavouring to prejudice the Pope against him with a view to the suppression of his monastery, or at least the destruction of his reform. At the same time the " lay pope," Louis XIV, who had hitherto shown but little sympathy, gave unmistakable signs of his appreciation of La Trappe and its Abbot.

Meantime De Rancé's condition did not improve. The famous physician, M. Hamon, immortalised by Boileau, hearing of his illness, hurried from Paris to offer him his services. Poor man, he returned disillusioned. The Abbot received him most courteously, not, however, as a doctor, but as a guest. In answer to complaints about this, he wrote to a friend : " It is a rule of the house never to call in a doctor however ill one may be, but to depend on the physician whom Providence has sent us for the cure of our maladies. My brethren, I know, would not take scandal if, maintaining this rule in their regard, I had no scruple about violating it myself ; nevertheless I feel bound to put no unnecessary temptation in their way, particularly as there are others in the monastery much more ill than I. Although, by the grace of God, their disposition is now what it ought to be, still, considering the inconstancy of the human heart, and that there are twelve hours in the day, we know not what the future may manifest. My practice is : never to put a stumbling block in the way of the community, but rather to remove from their path whatever could in the least retard their progress." Twice during the year 1678 he was brought to death's door : on one of these occasions he believed his recovery was obtained miraculously through the prayers of a holy monk named Brother Basil. No sooner did he recover strength enough to rise from his sick-bed than it was again " business as usual."

" Who could believe it did he not witness it for himself ?" writes Le Nain. " This man who seems to live on suffering, and as if he had a body of adamant, or rather no body at all, is always in action from morning till night. He writes, he dictates letters, he composes treatises, he reforms religious houses, he confers with the brethren, he guides the eighty persons, novices and professed, who constitute his community, he regulates all that concerns their spiritual and corporal necessities, and still finds time for prolonged prayer. He visits the infirmary, from the infirmary he goes to the cloister in order to see how the brethren are occupied, from the cloister to the choir to assure himself that the Divine Office is being discharged with due reverence, from the choir to his cell where some brother is waiting to receive instruction or advice.

"And although he is so tired that he can scarcely

keep on his feet, hardly a day passes that he has not to visit the guest quarters also to entertain some visitor, or to transact some important business. Then to the confessional where he expends the residue of his energies. You will see him emerging thence in summer time bathed in perspiration, and in winter benumbed with cold, after the long sittings. For although he has appointed several confessors, the religious will have nobody but himself. He still holds chapter once a week. And at this principal function of his office in which he exhibits so extraordinary a gift for reproving, instructing, inflaming, he shows a degree of animation that surprises everybody. He insists on attending the Offices, in order to consecrate what remains of his voice to the chanting of the Divine praises with wonderful devotion. Even the hours destined for repose are not withdrawn from his vigilance. At the time when others are sleeping, he goes about the monastery, visits the court-yard, sees that every brother is where he ought to be. In one word, he wants to see everything for himself, to know at first hand all that passes in the house, as being obliged to render an account to Him in Whose name he governs. Was there ever witnessed zeal so indefatigable, such energy of soul in a body quite exhausted and racked with pain?''

With regard to the Abbot's lectures in chapter (which he delivered daily until sickness obliged him

to limit himself to one per week) Bossuet says :
" I have paid three or four visits to La Trappe in
company with Father de Mouchy of the Oratory,
in order to make a retreat. We used to listen
secretly to the exhortations which he made to the
monks in chapter after the Office of Prime. So
animated were they, so powerful, so touching, that
we could not restrain our tears. The religious
came forth from that room filled with a new fervour,
and pierced with sentiments of compunction so
extraordinary that nothing appeared impossible to
them."

When Abbot du Tertre made his next visitation
at La Trappe, in 1678, he found himself at a loss
for words to describe the atmosphere of peace and
harmony that enveloped the monastery and made
it a heaven upon earth. The religious, fearing they
would soon lose their beloved superior unless he
could be persuaded to moderate his austerities,
implored the visitor to exercise his authority for
that purpose. The result was that De Rancé was
put under obedience to the cellarer until his health
should be restored. His convalescent regime may
not appear very attractive : not being allowed
to attend the night Offices in choir, he rose at 3
a.m., recited Lauds, Matins having been said the
evening before, read a chapter of the New Testament, another of the Imitation, then went to the
church where he passed two and a half hours in

prayer before celebrating Mass. As for his food, a little milk was added to the coarse legumes and black bread. He only took an egg when in such a state as would mean an order to take meat in the case of a member of the community. And his work went on as before. As soon as his health permitted, he resumed the regular vigils and fasts and the attendance in choir, and added some particular mortifications, as if to make up for past indulgence.

The frequent deaths at La Trappe and the sickly appearance of the survivors attracted public attention and exposed the Abbot to a good deal of sharp criticism. A number of the bishops thought it time to intervene. The laborious lives of the religious, they said, demanded somewhat better food than Abbot de Rancé was providing : eggs at dinner and a little wine with some fish on festivals would do no harm to the soul and a world of good to the body ; the change, so far from injuring the reform, would rather help it by conserving the health of the community : where would the reform be if the monks of La Trappe died out in a generation ? They reminded the Abbot also that " the letter killeth," that mortification of the will is more important than mortification of the body. And they entreated him to be less a master than a father to his monks. " Permit me to say," he wrote in answer, " that if I added to the nourishment what you suggest, it would be necessary to send away two-thirds of the community and to close the gates of the monastery against the poor.[2] And as the poor are very numerous here, not to speak of the guests, my brethren and I have thought it better to continue to share our bread with them than to deprive them thereof by our living an easier and more pleasant life. True, ' the letter killeth,' when observed alone, and bodily exercises avail little ; but when endeavours are made to animate them with the right spirit, I assure you they become very useful and very beneficial. I may add that the Briefs I have obtained from the Sovereign Pontiff presuppose the austerity of our life, so that if we relaxed anything thereof the validity of the graces accorded us might be open to question.

" With regard to my own personal conduct, I can only say that it is quite different from your conception of it. My relations with my brethren have all the charity, all the tenderness which God requires of me, and which His grace enables me to

2 The Abbé Nicaise informed De Rancé that a certain person had described the Trappists as sluggards who lived at their ease, and had no pity for the poor. In his reply the Abbot said :—" You might have told the critic that, in addition to the 1,500 or sometimes 2,000 poor supported by our alms during the years of scarcity, we also sustain privately, by monthly pensions, all the families of the neighbourhood who are unable to work; that we receive (per annum) 4,000 guests, and maintain 80 monks, and all from an income of from 8,000 to 9,000 livres at most. And then you might have asked him to point out to you ten households, each with the same income, who together do anything approaching to what these sluggards accomplish."

put into them. I exercise severity in chapter, because that is the place destined for the correction of faults : but my severity ceases there, it does not go further."

As for the future of his monastery, " our destiny," he declared, " is in the hands of God, and I will venture to say that La Trappe is His work : did I think otherwise, I would not remain here a single instant. It will therefore have the duration assigned to it in His eternal decrees. If in past times our ancestors guided their conduct by considerations of what *might* befall, since everything is subject to change and decadence, nothing would have been attempted. The field of Jesus Christ would be as an arid desert, devoid of all grandeur and beauty. No, I can't believe that God wants us to moderate our austerities. We shall continue just so long as He has ordained for us. But, in any case, it would be better to see our institution deprived of existence at once than enduring at the price of fidelity." After some years, however, he found that, with all their goodwill, his monks were unable to fast until evening, and so he decided to have the community dinner never later than noon.

he decisions of the Holy See and those of the
ishops as the rules of my belief and my conduct.
have condemned all that the Church has
ondemned in her sense and in her spirit without
quivocation.'' And to another friend he wrote :
' Far from repenting of having signed the formula,
am ready to sign it again as often as my superiors
nay require.''

In the year 1660, as has been said, he visited
Mgr. Pavillon, Bishop of Aleth. Sometime after
is return he wrote as follows to a friend named
Madame de Saint-Loup :

'' I must tell you in all sincerity that my joy was
ull when I found him (Mgr. Pavillon) not only
iving according to the rules of strict morality and
pending himself in the task of teaching the faithful
of his diocese to do likewise, but also absolutely
submissive to the ordinances and decisions of the
Church. With a holy zeal he confirmed me in my
sentiments with regard to the same, and often said
o me that there can be neither peace nor salvation
except in hearkening and assenting to the pro-
nouncements of the Church with perfect docility.
He read to me some very strong protests against
signing the formula which were sent to him by
somebody. ' There could be nothing more learned,
nothing more eloquent,' he remarked, ' nevertheless my views remain unaltered and cannot be
affected by any force of argument.' He exhorted

me most earnestly to persevere in my submission. I assure you I was delighted at this, and I regarded the counsel of this holy Bishop as a powerful help to me against the efforts of those who hold the opposite opinion. Let me tell you a remarkable circumstance. The first time he spoke to me about the signing of the formula was some days after my arrival at Aleth. On the day preceding my departure he had two chairs brought three hundred paces from the house to the bank of a mountain torrent where, after two hours' conversation, he repeated what I have already said on this subject, conjuring me to remain steadfast in the sentiments in which he found me, despite all the attempts that might be made, and all the arguments that might be adduced to pervert me. By the grace of God I have been faithful, and faithful I will continue to my last breath."

Would that Pavillon himself had remained equally faithful! Alas! he, so full of zeal to save others, was not able to save himself. Who could have believed that this Bishop, so pious, so austere, so faithful in preaching submission to the Church, was to become known in a year or two as one of the boldest and most obstinate of the Jansenistic leaders? He stands out as another melancholy illustration of the words of St. Paul: "He that thinketh himself to stand, let him take heed lest he fall" (I Cor. x, 12). But of all the many beautiful could no longer weep over one's sins without being suspected of heresy. If he practised austerities, as he did, it was not from the conviction that God was what the heretics tried to make Him, an extortionate creditor, a celestial Shylock. His penance had for object, of course, the expiation of sin, but it was also designed to engender, conserve, and develop the virtue of charity which must always remain in this life " a lily amongst thorns," the protecting thorns of penitential practices.

Still another circumstance tending to bring suspicion on De Rancé's faith was his well-known dislike of the Jesuit theology and spiritual direction. He expressed himself strongly on the subject, but not more strongly than other eminent writers, before his time and since, whose orthodoxy nevertheless has never been called in doubt. Nearly a century earlier good Catholics, such as Bañez and De Lemos, denounced Molinism (the Jesuit system of theology) to the Spanish Inquisition as involving heretical doctrines. The Abbot of La Trappe never went so far as that. His contemporary, Bossuet, the Eagle of Meaux, had as little liking for the Jesuit direction and doctrines as he, yet nobody accused him of heresy on that account. Jansenism and Molinism did not seem to either of them contradictorily opposed ; it was possible, they thought, to find a medium between the two systems. " I am neither a Molinist nor a Jansenist," said the

Abbot in his famous letter to Marshal Bellefonds, to which we shall have to refer again. "But if anyone desires to know what my opinions are concerning the points in dispute, I have never held any other than those of St. Thomas."

But that which beyond anything else gave colour to the accusations against his orthodoxy, and exposed him to a hurricane of abuse, was his letter to the Duke de Brancas in 1676. The Jansenist leaders had all signed the formula. In 1669 Clement IX spoke with joy of the assurance he had received "concerning the real and complete obedience with which they had sincerely subscribed the formula, condemning the five propositions without any exception or restriction, according to all the senses in which they had been condemned by the Holy See." The Duke above-named, on a visit to La Trappe, told the Abbot of the suspicion entertained by many touching the sincerity of the Jansenists' submission. In reply the Abbot said that, since the Sovereign Pontiff was satisfied with the manner in which they submitted and had no doubt as to their good faith, it would be very uncharitable for others to presume to judge them. His words were distorted, and thus given to the public. The misrepresentation was so serious that he felt obliged to write to De Brancas on the subject. After recalling what had passed between them he continues : —

" It is impossible that God should call either you or me to account for abstaining from judging our brothers, since neither of us has either the character or the office which would qualify us to judge ; but the opposite course of conduct might very easily involve us in guilt, howsoever pure our intentions. If they who have the authority or the obligation to pass judgment on others should chance to make a mistake, after applying themselves to the investigation of the matter with all care and diligence, they may hope to be pardoned by God Who knows the honesty of their purpose. But should this misfortune befall those who, without mission or necessity, usurp the office of judge, they have nothing to expect but rigorous chastisement ; by intruding into a position to which they have not been called, they deserve that God should abandon them to their own blindness. I assure you, Monsieur, that, for myself, I feel in nowise tempted to judge my brethren, because, on the one hand, I remember the threat of Jesus Christ to punish with everlasting torments even a comparatively light offence against one's brother, and, on the other, I regard myself as being at every instant about to appear before His Judgment-seat. I am persuaded that in matters such as those in question the safest way is to remain in silence and submission. It is also, of course, the way that will satisfy neither of the parties ; but so long as I

please God and do His Will I do not worry much
about the manner in which men may judge of my
conduct. . . . . I confess to you, Monsieur, that
I cannot help wondering at the blindness of the
majority of men who think no more of calling a
person a heretic or a schismatic than of saying that
he looks pale or sickly." Then speaking of the
reconciled Jansenists, he adds : " I should believe
myself guilty of an injustice were I to suspect their
orthodoxy. They are now in the communion and
in the bosom of the Church. She regards them as
her children, and consequently I am bound to
consider them as my brethren. . . . . I am convinced
that they have no bad doctrines."

These last words, in particular, rather intensified
than allayed the storm. They were taken out of
their context and made to look like a profession of
faith in Jansenism. But it should be remembered
that he had twice signed sworn declarations of his
belief that the five propositions which constituted
the soul of Jansenism were heretical in the sense
of their author. Therefore, what he meant in the
letter was that the *converted* Jansenists (of whom
he was speaking) held no bad doctrines, in other
words, that their abjuration had been sincere.

To explain away the misunderstanding and to
leave no room for doubt as to his position, he wrote
another long letter to Marshal Bellefonds : —

" I feel obliged to address you, Monsieur, on

the subject of the reports which have been put in circulation concerning me, but for which my conduct, by the grace of God, has never given occasion. My purpose is not to clear my reputation in your eyes, for you never doubted me and have always done me justice. I only wish to enable you to inform inquirers just where I stand and have always stood in regard to the questions disputed—that is, if you judge it right to do me this favour.

" Let me say, then, Monsieur, that since my retirement from the world I have never belonged to any party save that of Jesus Christ and His Church. I have watched this contest with pain of heart, but have taken no share in it beyond afflicting myself before God and weeping at the foot of the altar, as I beheld the children with their disputes rending the soul of their common Mother. . . . . I have always believed it my duty to submit to those whom God has placed over me as superiors and fathers. I mean the Pope and my Bishop. I have done what they desired of me, and I have signed the formula concerning the propositions of Jansenism without restriction and without reserve. So great has been my precaution to hold myself aloof from controversy that not only have I abstained from discussing the matters in dispute, but I have allowed no information concerning them to enter the community. None of my religious has ever opened his mouth to ask about either the questions or the persons connected with the dispute. I have kept aloof from fear of engaging in something out of keeping with my profession as a monk, and capable of disturbing the repose of my solitude, remaining however in a resolution firm and constant to embrace with perfect submission the orders of the Pope and the decisions of the Church. As a result I can say that, whilst the rest of the world has been in a state of tumult, we in La Trappe have enjoyed profound peace."

Then after saying that there is as much danger in making the road to heaven too wide and smooth as too narrow and rugged, he turns to the slanderers of his faith : " What ! do they presume to say that my faith is not sound ? Is not this to accuse me of the most heinous of crimes ? No man certainly ought to believe with confidence or make public the sin of another unless he is quite sure the sin has been committed and that he is under obligation to make it known. Now, let me ask those who so easily give themselves the liberty and the right to pronounce on my faith, what necessity obliges them thereto and what assurance have they of what they affirm ? I defy them to cite a single sentence, a single word of mine which will bear a sinister interpretation. . . . . Let these critics know that, be their zeal and their intention what they may, not thereby shall they be justified when God shall exhibit their false justices in their true character, and punish slanderers and calumniators with as much severity as blasphemers and adulterers."

Bremond is shocked to find a religious so much concerned for his own reputation, " mingling the recriminations of personal rancour with this *apologia pro fide sua.*" But, as he ought to know, there never has been a servant of God who remained silent under accusations of heresy. We would here call attention to a very curious phenomenon. Anybody with a word to say against De Rancé, whether he be a militant Jansenist or a runaway monk, is accepted by Bremond as a qualified witness ; but should his testimony tend in the opposite direction, he is scornfully dismissed as a mere apologist. Thus of the Le Nain brothers, the monk is considered as undeserving of any credit, although he lived more than thirty years in the most intimate relations with the holy Abbot, whilst the uncompromising Jansenist, Tillemont, merits to be called " the reliable Tillemont " when he testifies to the faith of De Rancé. Again, Bossuet thought so much of the letter to Marshal Bellefonds that he had it printed and published, thereby in a manner making its contents his own. What says our critic to that ? He involves the Eagle in his accusation of Jansenism ! " Surely thou also art one of them for even thy speech doth discover thee." One wonders how Pope Innocent XI managed to escape.

CHAPTER XVII.

Publication and Reception of the " De la Sainteté et des Devoirs de la Vie Monastique "—Trouble with the Premonstratensians, with the Carthusians and with the Congregation of St. Maur— Controversy with Mabillon — The illustrious Maurist visits La Trappe—His Impressions—A Conspiracy—A scurrilous Lampoon—Madeleine Serre.

In the month of March, 1683, appeared De Rancé's *chef-d'œuvre,* entitled *De la Sainteté et des Devoirs de la Vie Monastique.* The work consists of twenty-three conferences dealing with all the various aspects and duties of life in the cloister. It was written for the exclusive benefit of the monks of La Trappe, and at their urgent and repeated solicitation. Bossuet having surreptitiously obtained a copy of the manuscript insisted on having it published. On its title page it bore a letter of recommendation signed by him, by the Bishop of Luçon, and the Archbishop of Rheims. The letter, which seems to have been penned by Bossuet, runs : " This work, treating of the sanctity and duties of the monastic life, contains a doctrine accurately derived from Holy Scripture and the tradition of the saints. The reading of it will discover to monks the obligations and the perfection of the angelic state to which they have been called. It will prove not less profitable to people in the world by making them understand, from the austerities and humiliations practised in the cloister, how great is the corruption in which we live, how deeply the poison has penetrated our hearts, and how violent and incessant must be our efforts against ourselves if we hope not merely to prevent the growth of vicious habits but to pluck them up by the roots. The heretics will be confounded in presence of so solid a justification of the monastic institute which has become the object of their dislike simply because it is too far above their capacity. And assuredly they will show themselves exceedingly obstinate if they do not feel obliged to confess that God is truly in that holy house where such sublime teaching is not only inculcated with energy but faithfully reduced to practice."

The Bishop of Grenoble, our old friend, Le Camus, gave the work a separate letter of approbation. " It used to be said formerly," he writes, " that one should have lived like St. John Climacus so as to be able to compose his divine *Ladder of Perfection*. The same can be said of the author of this book. Five years ago I had the consolation both to hear from his lips and to see put in practice the grand and holy maxims which are contained in his volume, so that what is written in these pages is but the expression of his thoughts and actions. I have read the work attentively. Everything in it, so far as I can judge, is calculated to edify, and full of the Spirit of God. The sentiments are noble and elevated, and on the whole, it gives one a sublime conception of the religious life.''

With regard to the style of the work, we shall ask Chateaubriand, surely a competent judge, to give us his impressions of it. ''What is this new work which the Eagle of Meaux has covered under his wings? Its language has all the harmonies of the organ, full and majestic. One moves through its pages as through a basilica whose rose-windows are ablaze with the shimmering light of the sun. Oh, what a wealth of imagination in a work wherein, from its character, one would least expect to find it! Light and shade have had more to do with the erection of religious edifices than the hand of man. The perusal of De Rancé's work will convince those who need to be convinced that our language is indebted to him for a very beautiful book. Its first appearance was followed by an interval of profound silence, the silence of astonishment and admiration.''

As to the results of its publication, Bossuet exultantly wrote to the author: '' The book has produced all the good effects I had anticipated. It has done great good everywhere. You ought to return due thanks to God for giving you so happy an inspiration. Your doctrine is one against which the gates of hell shall not prevail, because it is founded on the rock." "No book within the memory of man," writes Lefèvre d'Ormesson, "has won for itself greater esteem at court, amongst the people, in the upper circles of society. But that would be little, if it had not at the same time produced inestimable fruits of virtue whereof I am myself a witness." Monsieur de Barillon, French ambassador at the English court, declared he "had never read a book which contained doctrine at once so solid and so beautifully and nobly expressed," and he used it to good purpose against the Anglican divines. The Abbé Nicaise demanded its immediate translation into Latin " so that the whole world may participate in the treasure of good it contains." These are but a few of the many testimonies to the excellent results the book produced.[1]

But it also produced other and less desirable results. The author describes with much force and

---

[1] This book so sponsored and so received has merited nothing but anger and contempt from M. Henri Bremond. He is quite indignant with Bossuet and his brother-bishops for lending the authority of their names to "an astonishing piece of humbug," which he would have placed on the Index whither, so he says, many less offensive publications have found their way. Commenting on the work, he affirms that De Rancé regarded " thinking as the heretic's original sin." Chapter and verse, please? This is a most serious charge which requires to be fully substantiated. It is a more serious charge than the charge of Jansenism, for if

freedom the decadent condition of monasticism i
his own day. This naturally aroused indignation i
nearly all the old Orders, his own not excepted. A
the next General Chapter the Abbot of Citeau:
denounced the book in the strongest terms a:
defamatory and as tending to create further division
in the Order; he demanded the removal of certai
passages. De Rancé made a successful defence
The Premonstratensians complained of the worl
because some of their number after reading it fel:
dissatisfied with their own Institute and entered
La Trappe. It was the same with the Carthusians
A member of that Order asked permission to join De
Rancé's community. Dom Innocent le Masson, Prio
of La Grande Chartreuse, and Superior-Genera
of the Order, learning that this religious had beer
reading *De la Sainteté et des Devoirs de la Vie
Monastique,* banished from his communities a book
which he described as " little calculated to edify,
but rather capable of disturbing consciences, of
making souls lose their simplicity and the right way
by the infusion of excessively rigorous ideas, the

the Abbot of La Trappe ever said anything of the
kind—of course, he didn't—he thereby declared orthodoxy antagonistic to reason. The same critic avers
that there has never been a mind more shallow than De
Rancé's : his own book, *Abbé Tempête,* stands as solid demonstration of the opposite. The Abbot of La Trappe desired
to gratify his self-conceit without losing his reputation for
humility; he always tried to make it appear that his writings
were published against his will, whereas in reality he composed for publication, such is the opinion of Bremond, " and
sure he is an honourable man."

fruit of an inflamed and extravagant zeal.'' The
Abbot of La Trappe, urged by Le Camus and other
friends to justify himself, firmly refused. Four years
later, when the matter had been almost forgotten,
Le Masson renewed the attack in the preface to
his *Annales*. This time De Rancé could not help
replying to his critic, which he did in a letter
addressed to Le Camus. The question in dispute
was this : whether or not the Carthusians of the
seventeenth century had in any respect degenerated
from the strict observance of their primitive constitutions. It hardly gave scope for debate.

The *De la Sainteté* had its critics also in the
Benedictine Congregation of St. Maur. Every son
of Citeaux venerates the name of Dom Jean
Mabillon, who employed all the resources of his
genius and learning for the glorification of St.
Bernard. This illustrious scholar felt it his duty to
challenge some of De Rancé's statements. He
concluded his criticisms with the words : '' These
reflexions are rather doubts which have suggested
themselves to me than real difficulties that I would
oppose to an excellent and useful book. And in
committing them to writing I protest that I have
nothing but esteem for the work and its author and
for the community of saints under his government.
I often pray for their welfare, and for that of the
great servant of God who directs them.'' A
courteous critic this. *O si sic omnes!*

Later on, after De Rancé had published his *Eclaircissements,* as a supplement to the *De la Sainteté* and designed to answer some difficulties arising out of this latter work, the erudite Maurist, in a book entitled *Traité des Etudes Monastiques,* controverted his opinion according to which monks should restrict their studies to Holy Scripture and the writings of the Fathers. The Abbot replied with energy. Despite all the arguments and reasons to the contrary, he writes : '' I am still persuaded that the reading of profane authors does not suit the denizens of the cloister. I too read the classics before my retirement into solitude. Since that time I have on three or four occasions opened Homer, Theocritus, and some of the other tragic poets, but only to put them away immediately, because my conscience told me that such lectures were not proper for a monk. Others may have different views, but mine is such as I have just expressed, and I find it impossible to entertain any other.''

He then describes the effect the reading of Livy produced on his mind : for whole days together he could think of nothing but Hannibal and Scipio and their wars, prayer or recollection was no longer possible. '' You may tell me that this should be attributed to my weakness. Granted. But I believe there are a good many like me.''

Mabillon published a rejoinder to which the Abbot

was ready to reply when something happened that put an end to the friendly discussion. The champion of monastic studies paid a visit to La Trappe. So gentle and humble did he show himself that De Rancé had not the heart to continue the controversy, and his reply remained unpublished.

Mabillon gave his impressions of La Trappe in a letter to a priest of his own Congregation. The following extracts will be of interest :—

" We were received with every possible mark of cordiality and friendship by the Rev. Father Abbot and the community, whom one cannot behold without being edified. We assisted at the Office of Matins. It lasted four hours. The pauses in each verse at this Office are lengthened out to the space of an Ave, but at the other canonical hours they are shorter than we make them. The movement is fairly brisk, except at the Salve Regina, which takes a quarter of an hour. As for the chant, it could not be excelled. There are some very good voices amongst the eighty choir religious in the community. We counted twelve novices : Augustinians, Cordeliers, Oratorians, and members of other Orders. All these wear the tonsure of their first profession along with the novice's habit.

" I have conversed four times with the Father Abbot. The first time there was no reference to our dispute. On the second occasion, Father Abbot began by saying he hoped he had not in any way hurt me by anything he said during the controversy. At these words I embraced him. We both of us fell upon our knees, and thus I answered that his writings against me had in nowise diminished the regard and veneration I felt for him. He then said that when a person is penetrated with an important truth, he is very apt to express himself with more energy than is proper. But he begged me to feel assured that he entertains the greatest possible esteem and affection for our entire Congregation, and myself in particular.''

As to the merits of this debate about monastic studies, most people consider that Mabillon had the better case. Such, however, was not the opinion of the Church historian Fleury, nor of the Archbishop of Paris, Mgr. de Noailles, nor of the more recent Church historian, Rohrbacher, called by Lacordaire the St. Thomas of ecclesiastical history. According to the latter, the Maurist proceeded on the assumption that the Abbot wished to interdict all kinds of study in the cloister, which certainly was not the case : hence all his arguments went wide of the mark.[2] The Protestant philosopher, Leibnitz, considered that each of the disputants was right in his own sense : there was an *ignoratio elenchi*.

Meantime, the holy Abbot's health continued to be for the community he directed a cause of most anxious solicitude. They found him a good father

2 Hist. Univers. de l'Egl. Cath. t. xxvi., pp. 491, 509.

indeed, but a bad patient. A plan suggested itself ;
they hatched a conspiracy against him ; and whilst
he remained blissfully ignorant of what was afoot,
a letter, signed by the prior, the sub-prior, and the
cellarer, was dispatched to Rome, containing the
request that the Pope should place Abbot de Rancé
under obedience to the signatories in all that
regarded his health. Cibo, the Cardinal-Secretary,
answered the conspirators as follows : — " Very
Rev. Fathers, His Holiness has received with much
pleasure the letter you sent him, a letter which
testifies so eloquently to the love and attachment you
have for the wonderful man whom God has given
you as your abbot. He has spoken with admiration
of your care and solicitude for your superior's health,
and of your purpose to exercise yourselves still
longer in the penitence ordained by the Gospel,
and to fortify yourselves therein more and more
under the holy discipline which Abbot de Rancé
has established in your house. He rejoices at the
view of your zeal and fervour, especially in times of
so much laxity and disorder. However, His Holiness believes that your Abbot, out of respect for
the commandments of God which do not permit us
to destroy our bodies, will for the future have more
care of his health, still so necessary to the prosperity
of the house. He even charges you to admonish
him thereof and to speak to him on the subject, in
his (the Pope's) name and authority, as often as

you may judge necessary. This is what the Holy
Father has ordered me to write in answer to your
letter. In testimony of his particular affection, he
imparts to you through me his paternal benediction.
For myself, venerable Fathers, I entreat you to
assist me with your prayers before God, as I do
not fail to solicit all kinds of favours for you.''

The conspiracy did not prosper quite as much as
was hoped, but well enough to make the conspirators happy.

The year 1685 witnessed a new publication from
the pen of De Rancé, a translation of the Greek
Father, St. Dorotheus. Before giving his manuscript to the printer, he sent it to Cotelier, professor
of Greek at College Royal, and one of the best
Hellenists of his time, to get his opinion on the
rendering of certain obscure passages. The professor found nothing to alter, and not knowing the
writer's name, wrote on the margin of the MS. :
'' The person who has consulted me concerning
these difficulties is a better Greek scholar than I
am.'' The following notice of the work appeared in
the *Journal des Savants,* December 2nd, 1685 :
'' No one was more capable of giving us this
translation than he who at the age of ten could
already render and expound Homer with the skill
of a master and who, between twelve and thirteen,
gave the public a commentary on Anacreon which
met with a warm welcome. The present work, we

feel assured, will prove not less successful, since
the rendering has undoubtedly preserved all the
beauties of the original, and one experiences therein
that unction and simplicity, so appealing to souls,
and so characteristic of the writings of St.
Dorotheus."

The elevation of his friend Bishop le Camus to
the cardinalate in 1686 greatly rejoiced the Abbot.
" It is true," he wrote, " the honour done to the
Bishop of Grenoble has given me the greatest satisfaction, not only for personal reasons, but also for
reasons relating to the public good. Assuredly it
is a glory for him to have been indebted for his
elevation to merit alone, and in no degree to
intrigues or manœuvres. For, of a truth, God
prepared him for this dignity by exercising him
sixteen years in the exact and faithful discharge of
the duties of the episcopate. All persons of goodwill
must feel consoled at the news."

At this time there was circulating in France a
book entitled : *Les véritables Motifs de la conversion de l'abbé de la Trappe, avec quelques ré-
flexions sur sa vie et sur ses écrits, ou Entretiens
de Timocrate et de Philandre sur un livre qui a
pour titre: Les Saints Devoirs de la Vie Monastique.* It bore neither the name of the author nor
that of the printer. And for a very intelligible
reason. The book was a most slanderous and
scurrilous attack on De Rancé. His early life was

depicted in the blackest colours, the story of the Duchess's severed head was recited with a setting of ghastly details, his retirement from the world was represented as the effect not of grace or of virtue, but of spite and despair. But although he withdrew from the world, the author goes on, he could not leave the world in peace; he continued to be the cause of commotion and confusion by means of his writings. One of these books, especially, did a great deal of mischief by its misrepresentations and exaggerations of everything connected with monastic life—the voice indeed is the voice of Henri Bremond, yet it is certain he was not the author of this earlier *Abbé Tempête*. The libeller had even the meanness to say that the famishing poor could get nothing from the well-fed Abbot of La Trappe beyond good wishes and the promise of prayer, whereas everybody knew how De Rancé and his community were starving themselves in order to find means to succour the indigent. Careful and long-continued inquiries discovered the author of this precious volume in the person of one Daniel le Larroque, a convert from Protestantism, who had got the work printed in Cologne.

This was not by any means the only attempt made on De Rancé's character by the masked banditti. We have already referred to the forged letter wherein the Abbot appears as a shameless trafficker in holy things. The publication of the *De la Sainteté* was followed by the appearance of an anonymous lampoon, not quite so bad as Larroque's, but bad enough to cause the authorities to forbid its circulation. Later on, another device was adopted. The irritable King Louis XIV received letters, signed by monks of La Trappe, which threatened him with the vengeance of God unless he did so-and-so. This appeared all the more serious from the fact that De Rancé had shown great kindness and hospitality to the Duchess de Guise at a time when she lay under the displeasure of her royal cousin. Investigation, however, proved the letters to be malicious forgeries.

In the month of May, 1682, an event occurred at a place called Lareu in the parish of Alan, diocese of Comminges, which gave origin to a movement similar to those of La Salette and Lourdes. A little shepherdess, named Madeleine Serre, twelve years of age, happened to fall into a bramble-covered ditch, whilst tending her flock. In her terror she invoked the holy name of Jesus. Immediately a beautiful Lady dressed in luminous white appeared at the edge of the ditch and lifted her out. The Lady introduced herself as the Mother of Jesus. She bade the child inform the parish priest that she wished the foundation of a chapel to be laid in that spot, and that a stranger would come to complete the edifice. To accredit her

ambassadress she told Madeleine to proclaim that a
nearby spring would be found possessed of healing
properties.   Several other children, employed in
the same humble occupation as Madeleine, saw the
Lady conversing with her, but were too far distant
to hear what was said.

The parish priest paid no attention to the child's
story ; but the people flocked to the fountain where
miraculous   cures,   multipled   beyond   number,
rewarded their simple faith. After a careful examination of these prodigies, the Bishop, Mgr. de
Rechigne-Voisin de Guron, authorised the erection
of a large cross at the place of the alleged
apparition.   Some beginning was made with the
construction of a small chapel, but the undertaking
seems to have been abandoned very soon. Things
remained thus for several years.

In 1688 a novice at La Trappe named Brother
Dositheus—in the world, Pierre Catieni—felt an
irresistible conviction that he was the person
destined to fulfil Our Lady's wish, and to complete
the chapel. His superiors, believing him to be the
victim of an illusion, gave him no encouragement,
rather the contrary.   But as he persisted, and
showed himself a young man of prudence and solid
piety, they came at last to the view that the urge
might possibly be an inspiration from heaven, and
so they counselled the novice to follow the call.
When Brother Dositheus presented himself before

Mgr. de Guron, with the request for permission to erect the chapel, the good Bishop was sorely embarrassed. He deferred his answer until he had consulted the Abbot of La Trappe. In his letter to the Abbot he expressed his fear of diabolical illusion. De Rancé set his mind at ease. What clearer evidence could you possibly have, he said, that the work is of God than this multitude of miraculous cures and the moral reformation of your diocese? If the devil be its author, then assuredly is his kingdom divided against itself and Satan is striving to cast out Satan.

Fortified with episcopal sanction, Br. Dositheus set to work. In a comparatively short time he witnessed the solemn consecration not of a small chapel but of a large church, served by a number of holy priests. The Bishop desired to put it in charge of Trappist monks, but De Rancé considered the suggestion impracticable. The church was dedicated to Our Lady and St. Bernard, and continued to be one of the most venerated sanctuaries in France down to the outbreak of the Revolution. Madeleine entered a Cistercian convent, and there made a happy end.

CHAPTER XVIII.

Conversions—Controversy with Bishop du Plessis-Praslin—" Explication de la Règle de Saint-Benoît "—Rumour of Cardinalitial Honours for De Rancé—Another Plot.

IN the midst of his many tribulations, the Abbot of La Trappe found much to console him. After the publication of his works on the monastic state, he had the joy of leading back to God two noble ladies who had spent many a year in that " far country " of husks and swine and spiritual hunger. The Princess Anne de Gonzague de Clèves, widow of the Prince Palatine Edward, abandoning the piety which had characterised her youth, began to live only for pleasure. At length grace touched her heart by means of a most extraordinary dream, the story of which may be read in Dubois, *Histoire,* t. 11, pp. 56—60. She immediately placed herself under the direction of De Rancé, and by faithfully following his counsels attained to a height of perfection rarely witnessed in the world. It was of her Cardinal de Retz declared that she had more capacity for government than the English Queen Elizabeth. She wrote an account of her conversion

at the request of the Abbot. Another remarkable
conversion of the time was that of the Countess
de la Fayette, *la grande Madame,* one of the
leading lights of Europe. The Abbot of La Trappe
gave her guidance and encouragement whilst she
made the long and weary journey from religious
scepticism back to the faith of her childhood. In
the days of her wandering he wrote to her thus :
" I have seen so many prodigals returning from
that land afar off that I cannot but hope you will
yet be one of the number. God has endowed you
so richly with noble natural qualities of mind and
heart, of probity and honour, that I cannot believe
you will refuse the supernatural gifts and graces
without which all the rest would be of no avail. We
shall pray with all earnestness for your entire conversion."

The reader—if he has had the patience to follow
us so far—will remember Monsieur de Saint-Louis,
the military officer who wished to employ the un-
canonical means of the sword for the reformation of
the primitive Trappists. He prospered in his profession, attained the rank of brigadier, and enjoyed
the confidence and friendship of King Louis and
the great Turenne. But amidst the excitements
and alarms of war he never forgot De Rancé ; the
impression made on his mind by the Abbé's per-
sonality remained uneffaced and ineffaceable. In
1685 he resolved to quit the army and to spend the

rest of his life in making atonement for his sins under the direction of the Abbot of La Trappe. When his purpose became known, some charitable friend warned him of the risk he was running in choosing for his '' sky pilot '' a man suspected of Jansenism. This completely upset the officer, for he detested that heresy and would have nothing to do with its advocates. But, being a man of courage and candour, he decided before seeking another retreat, to question De Rancé himself on the subject. He has left us a very interesting account of the interview :

'' The first time I saw the Abbot I opened my mind to him. He listened to what I had to say with the utmost gentleness and tranquillity, praised me for being so frank, and blessed the good God for making His Will known to me and confirming me in my vocation. Then he said : ' As for the report that I am a Jansenist, I am nothing of the kind. I may tell you, though, that some of my friends have endeavoured to secure my adhesion to the sect, but all their efforts have been useless. My enemies, intent on poisoning the mind of the King against me, have put out that report. This I learned from Marshal Bellefonds, and so was obliged to write him a letter which may be regarded as my profession of faith.' ''

De Saint-Louis lived thirty years as a hermit at La Trappe, universally admired for his humility and spirit of mortification. When his last hour came in 1714, he thanked God for having made him live a little while in the obscurity of the cloister before making his descent into the obscurity of the tomb.

The dull days of 1688 were enlivened by a very animated controversy between the Abbot of La Trappe and the Bishop of Tournay, none other than Mgr. du Plessis-Praslin, who, as Bishop of Comminges, had been one of De Rancé's counsellers in the period following his conversion. The dispute originated thus. Abbess de Choiseul who governed the Cistercian convent of Du Sauveur, near Laon, was advised by her physician and permitted by her superiors to return to her family until her health, undermined by a conscientious and zealous discharge of the duties of her office, should be restored. Mgr. du Plessis-Praslin, her uncle, strongly urged her to follow the doctor's advice. She had a scruple about doing so, and (*suadentediabolo*) consulted Abbot de Rancé on the question. No need to say what counsel she received from him. He reminded her of her obligations to perpetual enclosure. A letter written by him to a third party, in which he mentions this matter, and expresses his surprise at the conduct of the Bishop, fell into the same Bishop's hands. He felt hurt and annoyed.

" As for me," he wrote, " I do not believe that piety should be pitiless. One ought rather to die,

I admit, than do anything evil of its nature. But to refuse permission to an Abbess, who governs her community with perfect prudence, to take the waters that would establish her health, and to prefer to let her die or languish in a condition of absolute inutility rather than allow her home for a month or two : this is a firmness I cannot approve of. Nor should I call it firmness but cruelty and inhumanity were I not speaking of a man for whose merit I have a boundless veneration and for his person a boundless love." In his reply the Abbot recalled how " Saint Francis de Sales, the gentlest and most modern of saints, forbade the nuns of the Visitation to leave their cloisters in order to go to watering places on account of any maladies whatsoever, declaring that they should think more of their obligations than of their health. And Mother de Chantal, who was also a saint,[1] deposed a superioress of her Order for going to the water, although that was the only remedy which could save her life, and although she acted in obedience to her physician and with her Bishop's approval. In short, the salvation of their souls has always been to the saints a matter of more importance than the health of their bodies. You surely cannot accuse of cruelty or inhumanity one who has more concern to sanctify men than to make their lives pleasanter."

[1] M. Bremond says that De Rancé admitted no saints since St. Bernard's time, a statement as true as many another in his book.

That did not end the discussion, however, for
the Bishop of Tournay would not acknowledge himself worsted so soon. Whilst the controversy continued, one of De Rancé's own sisters in religion
was recommended by her doctors and superiors to
take a holiday at the seaside for the benefit of her
health. By her confessor's advice she consulted her
brother. His answer was prompt and straight to
the point. He loved her dearly, but that should
not and would not prevent him from speaking to
her as his conscience directed. As for going to the
seaside to recruit her enfeebled health, had she
not made a vow to live and die within the limits
of the enclosure? Very well : let her keep it. So
the poor Sister had to stay at home. The Abbess
also, it appears, lost her outing.

In 1689 the Abbot of La Trappe published
another important work : *Explication de la Règle de
Saint-Benoît,* furnished with letters of approbation
from the Archbishop of Rheims and the Bishop of
Meaux. According to Bossuet, " the Rule of St.
Benedict, wherein the monks ought to find the will
of God in their regard, could not have a more
capable interpreter than the author of this commentary, in which there is nothing that is not in
harmony with the Catholic, Apostolic and Roman
faith, nothing but what is redolent of the spirit of
the ancient solitaries of whom the world was not
worthy." All the austerity of the great Abbot's

mind appears in his interpretation of the Rule. Every word is taken in its literal sense, every ordinance considered almost as fixed and immutable as the prescriptions of the natural law. He would have the Rule observed in the monasteries of the seventeenth century with just the same exactitude as it was in St. Benedict's, conceding nothing to the altered conditions of society, nothing to the weakened constitution of men. As for dispensations, " by reason of the hardness of men's hearts " they had been granted, " but from the beginning it was not so." And he wanted to get back to the beginning.

He allows, however, that religious who make use of mitigations can still sanctify themselves, provided such mitigations have been authorised by the Church. But whilst insisting on the obligation of silence, solitude, manual labour, and the other austerities prescribed by Rule, he recognises that these are after all only a means to an end, which is charity. Silence is worse than useless, unless when the lips are kept closed the soul interiorly converses with God, solitude to be profitable must be filled with the presence of God, and whilst the hands are busy with spade or mattock the heart and the thoughts should be uplifted to Him. "Your watchings," he wrote, " must be spiritualised : you must come forth from your couches as from your tombs, and your souls, shaking off all languor and drowsiness, must accompany every movement of your tongues whilst you chant the divine praises. It is not enough to fast simply because fasting is enjoined by obedience, we ought to fast from the conviction that our sins have rendered us unworthy not alone of the food forbidden, but also of that which is allowed. And when engaged at manual labour, we must try to sanctify that exercise by our reflections and by an express intention to imitate, at least during these few hours, the laborious life led by Our Lord Jesus Christ during the whole period of His mortal existence. If any of you should happen to be appointed to some abject office in the monastery, he will find comfort in the thought that humiliations accepted and endured in the proper spirit merit as their recompense everlasting exaltation ; besides, a review of his past life will convince him that he has no right to expect anything but contempt and confusion. Surely dust and ashes cannot reasonably complain when blown about and scattered by the winds of heaven. If Jesus Christ, Who had only the image and appearance of sin, was nevertheless overwhelmed with inconceivable shame and humiliation, ' the reproach of men and the outcast of the people ' : what degree of ignominy can be considered too much for us who bear not only the image of sin, but its guilt and its horror ? Such. my brethren, are the dispositions in which we ought to pass our lives.'' As for particular humiliations, pride is an aposteme which poultices cannot cure ; it must be lanced. No humility, without humiliations, says St. Bernard.

The *Explication* got an enthusiastic reception from the reading public. De Rancé's rich imagination and charming style could quicken into palpitating life and clothe with flesh and beauty even the dry bones of moral precepts. Amongst the letters of congratulation received by the author was one from the scholarly Pellisson. " It is my custom," wrote the distinguished convert, " to return thanks for a bad book as soon as I get it, and for a good book only after I have read it. The more I study your book—I have it read to me even during meals—the more I find to admire in it. Not seldom have I felt an impulse to rise from table and hurry away to La Trappe to join in the exercises practised by the community. What particularly astonishes me is that you in the midst of your austerities can surpass us, men of the world, as much in polish as in piety, and write better than those who make writing their profession."

This year (1689) the report went about that Pope Innocent XI intended to raise the Abbot of La Trappe to the dignity of cardinal. Letters of felicitation poured in upon him from all sides. "The news whereof you speak," he wrote in answer to one of these, " has travelled round the world, and has come to my ears from fifty different quarters. But let me tell you that no power on earth can elevate me or make me more than I am either within or without my profession. I have the most evident reasons for thinking that God wants me to live and die in the state to which He has called me, and I must not listen to any other voice in preference to His. I believe this sentiment will merit your approval. The Pope entertains too high an opinion of me." " Far from accepting the episcopal or cardinalitial dignity," he replied to another, " I will never approve of such responsibilities being laid on me or on any other member of the Cistercian Order." And to Mgr. de Harlay, Archbishop of Paris, he said : " The only change possible or desirable so far as I am concerned is one of degradation. It has long been my wish to descend to the condition of a simple monk."

However, his own fears and the hopes of his friends were falsified by the event. When Innocent XI died unexpectedly on August 12th, the project died with him.

The same year saw the Abbot of La Trappe involved in very serious danger of another kind. A member of the chapter of Beauvais, disappointed at not being elected to some office, revenged himself upon the other canons by having them denounced as conspirators against the State. He addressed a number of incriminating letters in their names to the King's enemy, Prince William of Orange. Several of them were arrested and dragged in chains to Paris where they were incarcerated pending trial. Soon the report spread that the plot had been hatched in De Rancé's monastery, for some of the canons were his intimate friends. The situation seemed doubly serious in view of the suspicions of the Abbot's loyalty already entertained by the King. But before any action was taken against La Trappe, the forger acknowledged his crime and paid the penalty on the scaffold.

The Abbot of La Trappe enjoyed such prestige throughout the whole of France, and even beyond its frontiers, that every kind of question was being constantly referred to him for solution. Imagine Malebranche, the most distinguished philosopher of his generation, asking De Rancé for an explanation of the divining-rod ! Above all, imagine him getting it ! One would have expected the answer would be : *Retro me, Satana.* But no. The facts are these. A peasant in Dauphiné had the power of discovering by means of a forked switch springs of water and metal ores hidden in the bowels of the earth, and even, it was said, guilty consciences. The case was referred to Malebranche : he was asked to state if the thing could be done by natural means. Not being able to come to a decision, he wrote about the matter to Abbot de Rancé. Here is the reply he received :

" Monsieur, I have kept you a long time waiting for a disappointing answer to the letter you did me the honour to write me. I have read and re-read it, and submitted it to persons who have more wisdom than I. It is my opinion, then, that by mere natural force a rod may move itself when held over water or metal, and thus reveal their presence. That does not seem to me beyond the powers of nature, and is nothing more extraordinary than the movement of a needle that has been touched to a magnet. But that the rod should move in such a way as to point out a guilty person, or a boundary that has been changed, or that it should fail to function when the person holding it so desires—that would not admit of a natural explanation. For a criminal by his crime does not acquire any new physical quality, neither does a boundary stone by its removal. Nor can a purely physical force accommodate itself automatically to our intentions ; since it lacks both knowledge and liberty it must act always in the same manner, unless it is opposed by physical obstacles. But that is not so in the case you have described. As we must agree, therefore, that such phenomena cannot be explained naturally, they must be attributed either to the holy angels or to the demons. One can hardly conceive the angels as their authors, because one cannot conceive how God's honour is promoted by such ministrations. The same cannot be said of the demons who, in their malice, are always intent to seduce men by all kinds of impostures. . . . . Although the bending of the rod over water and metal can be naturally explained, I am convinced that in the present case it is due to the same diabolical power which controls it when it seems to exhibit freedom and intelligence. There is nothing more to say except to assure you that I take a deep interest in your work and pray that you may have the peace of God and perfect tranquillity. And do you in return remember me before the Lord."

CHAPTER XIX.

Quietism—De Rancé asked to oppose the new Heresy—Visitation of the Clairets—De Rancé dissuades Mgr. de Barillon from changing his Diocese—More Trouble—Still another Conspiracy—James II of England visits La Trappe.

SOME years before the death of Innocent XI and under cover of the Jansenistic controversy, another heresy, not less subtle but much more seductive, crept over the Alps from Italy and propagated itself silently through France. People called it Quietism. Its author was a Spanish priest named Michael de Molinos, born in 1627. According to his teaching, perfection consists in a state of absolute passivity : the perfect man no longer reasons, no longer desires or fears anything, heaven and hell not excepted, is completely indifferent to all that passes within him, neither troubles himself to banish temptation nor to excite devotion, and is so intimately united to God that he ceases to be responsible for his actions. In short, he becomes impeccable. Any sane mind can see at once how such a system would work out in practice. Moral depravity was its natural consequence. It did incalculable mischief in Italy and in certain parts of France. In vain Pope Innocent condemned it : the evil continued to spread. Rome wanted a man like St. Bernard or St. Dominic to combat this latest of heresies. The following letter from Cardinal Colloredo to a friend in France, who was also a friend of De Rancé's, will show us the man it had in view :

" Some persons who are eminent for piety and enjoy the full confidence of the Pope have charged me to make known to the Abbot of La Trappe that there has appeared at Rome and throughout Italy a kind of spirituality founded on what is called the Prayer of Quiet. It has wrought much evil and ruined a vast number of simple souls. It was hoped that the imprisonment of the priest De Molinos, regarded as the author of this prayer, would arrest the progress of the pestilence. But so far from losing ground, we behold it extending its conquests from day to day. All who love the Church, and all persons of note in this city, ardently desire that the Abbot of La Trappe, the only man of our age qualified to deal with errors of this kind, would give the support of his pen to the morality preached by Christ, and defend the doctrines of true mysticism against the impostures and novelties of the Quietists. Their principal work is the *Dux Spiritualis* of Molinos. If you cannot get the book in France, I shall have it sent to you. I consider this matter as

of the greatest importance. All with whom I have
spoken thereof believe that this is an occasion for
the Abbot to manifest the zeal of his burning heart
for the interests of holy Church. He must not be
allowed to decline the task, no matter what excuses
his humility may suggest. Once a general war has
been proclaimed, every citizen is bound to bear
arms. We all know what the saints of the desert
have done in the like circumstances. Were Saint
Antony, or St. Bernard—whom Abbot de Rancé so
loyally imitates—alive to-day, he would emerge
from his solitude to confront the seducers and would
not scruple to break his silence in defence of truth.
Do all in your power to persuade him to undertake
this work which would gloriously crown his penitential labours and stop up the source of an infinity of
evils. Both my friends and I await your answer with
impatience."

On the same subject Cardinal le Camus addressed
the holy Abbot : " A priest has written me to say
it is the general belief in Rome that you are the
only man in France capable of producing a solid
work on mental prayer, a work that would discredit
the Quietists' form of devotion and all the other
ill-regulated devotions so numerous in our day. It
is for you to judge if you are in a fit condition of
health for such an undertaking and if you deem it
necessary." Several other influential persons from
different parts appealed to the Abbot to exert him-

self in defence of Christian morality. But in his then state of health literary composition was out of the question. The pains of rheumatism, long familiar, had now become so intense and constant that he was kept always on the rack. Another competent writer came forward to undertake the task which he found too heavy. That other was the Bishop of Meaux, and his book bears the title, *Etats d'Oraison*. We shall have occasion to refer to it again.

In the year 1690, despite his grievous sufferings, the Abbot made a canonical visitation of a Cistercian convent in the diocese of Chartres, the community of which were called Clairets. He owed his appointment as Visitor to the urgent solicitations of the nuns themselves. And they received him as an angel from heaven. His parting address was so tender and touching that the whole community were moved to tears. The visitation produced lasting fruits of fervour and regularity. It so happened that the pious Abbess, Mother de Valençay, had not yet received the abbatial benediction, although installed more than two years. Through the influence of her aunt, the Princess de Meckelbourg, she obtained from the Abbot of Citeaux, authorisation for De Rancé to perform that ceremony. Although he did not feel too grateful for the honour, he had no option but to gratify her desire.

Mgr. Barrillon, Bishop of Luçon, to whose brother, the French ambassador in London, we have already made reference, wished to exchange his diocese for another. His principal reason for desiring a change was the state of his health which he hoped would improve in a more salubrious climate. Nevertheless, being a man of tender conscience, he had a scruple about the matter. He consulted the Abbot of La Trappe. The Abbot confessed that at first, yielding overmuch to human motives, particularly to his affection for the friend of many years, he thought he should approve of the change ; but when he looked at the question from God's point of view, he felt obliged to alter his opinion.

"Considering, then," he wrote, "what God requires of you, what the Church expects from you, and the edification you owe to the world, I cannot help thinking that you ought to remain where Divine Providence has placed you. Thus you will give a good example of which there has never been greater need than now, since we live in times when episcopal translations are so common that one may say the Church is kept in perpetual motion. In the second place, you know, Monseigneur, that Jesus Christ is the gate by which the shepherd ought to enter the sheepfold ; He has said that there are no legitimate pastors there save such as He has called. It is He Himself Who must give them their vocations. Now I cannot see how the facility which your influence gives you for changing to another diocese can be considered as the call of Christ. Hence, it would not be He Who sent you thither, Who gave you your mission, and there would be reason to fear that, far from finding there the repose you seek, you would experience nothing but regret and dissatisfaction. In the third place, remember it is God Who holds your destiny in His hands ; as Lord of life and death, He decides our lot, and multiplies our years as it pleases Him, independently of our care and diligence. Our foresight is so uncertain that we often run straight into the dangers we want to avoid ; and it happens not seldom that all our precautions only serve to bring the more surely upon us the evils they were designed to prevent. In a word, it is God Who has placed you where you are, it is He Who has espoused you to the church of Luçon. He has hitherto blessed your ministry there. Hence, I don't think your tender conscience will allow you any peace if, of yourself, you withdraw from the position He has assigned you. ' What therefore God hath joined together let not man put asunder.'

'' Such, Monseigneur, is my view of the matter, since you have requested me to lay it before you. I offer it with all submission to your better lights, for well I know that God is above all rules, and that

He speaks to His faithful servants and reveals to hem what He hides from others.''

The good Bishop took the advice tendered him and remained in Luçon.

His visitation of the convent of Clairets, so profitable to the nuns, yielded the Abbot of La Trappe a plentiful harvest of trouble. Like all canonical visitors he left with the community a written instruction and exhortation, called the " visitation card,'' which was to be read in public at stated times. Some of the religious admired his address so much that they made extracts and abstracts and sent them to their friends in the world. As a consequence, a number of manuscripts, completely misrepresenting the Abbot's mind, appeared in circulation. To correct the false impression made, he had no alternative but to get the card printed as it was written. It was like flinging a bone to hungry dogs : the critics pounced at once and with avidity upon the new publication. Three points gave occasion for a noisy exhibition of virtuous zeal. The Jansenists were indignant to find in the list of spiritual books recommended to the nuns by De Rancé the works of six Jesuit authors, and none of their own. Others complained that the list included Berniérès-Louvigny's treatise entitled *Chrétien Intérieur,* the Italian translation of which was said to have been condemned at Rome. But what chiefly aroused opposition was the Abbot's advice to the nuns to read no more of the Old Testament than the books of Psalms and Proverbs.

" Yes," he wrote to the Abbé Nicaise, who had informed him of the tempest his words had excited, " Yes, that is my opinion, and I wish the whole world to know it. You can tell the critics that if it be heresy, I too shall condemn it, but I shall wait until it has first been condemned by the Church. I am entirely convinced that there is nothing in what I have said that deserves ecclesiastical censure. Saint Basil told Chilon, a solitary of eminent virtue, that the reading of the Old Testament would rather hinder than help him. ' I do not deny,' he says, ' that in itself it is most holy, being the inspired word of God, but things in themselves good may be bad for us by reason of our human weakness.' Saint Nilus held the same opinion as St. Basil." Bossuet, in closing the controversy, agreed with the Abbot that the Old Testament should not be placed in the hands of all indiscriminately, yet believed that exceptions should be made in regard to persons of particular dispositions. This amendment De Rancé willingly accepted.

Scarcely had this tempest subsided when another began. A professed member of a certain religious Order, after many entreaties, after warning the Abbot that if he continued to refuse him he would be held accountable for his soul before God, obtained admission to the noviciate at La Trappe.

He had a papal Brief authorising his action, so that everything seemed in order. After five or six days he fled from the monastery and returned to his original house. To show he had not wasted his time whilst away from his brethren, he wrote a very lengthy account of his experiences in La Trappe. It all tended to prove that Abbot de Rancé was, despite his public disclaimers, a thorough-going Jansenist, and had made his monastery an asylum for the sect : he permitted no books to be read there save those written by Jansenists or defending their doctrines, and none but the heretics were welcomed at his door. In order to strengthen his case, he forged two letters, signing them with a lady's name. One was addressed to Father de la Chaise, the King's confessor, and informed him that the Abbot of La Trappe was a zealous supporter of Jansenism ; the other was directed to De Rancé himself : it warned him that Father de la Chaise intended to denounce him to the King as an enemy to the State, and urged him to save himself by instant flight. The " lady " remarked that, fearing her handwriting would be recognised and the letter intercepted, she had dictated it to a servant.

Louis XIV, to whom the matter was immediately reported, allowed himself to be deceived by an imposture which, one would have thought, could not have deceived a child. He demanded an explanation from the Abbot, also a list of the names of his religious and visitors, with particulars as to their profession, nationality, etc. In fact, De Rancé had no end of trouble to clear himself, notwithstanding the kind offices of the Archbishops of Paris and Rheims. If he failed, La Trappe would probably have shared the fate of Port Royal. However, the author of all the mischief repented of his crime, and made a full and public retractation. It was not from any personal ill-will to De Rancé he had acted, he said, but he had permitted himself to be made a tool of by others.

On the evening of November 24th, 1690, King James II, fresh from the debacle of the Boyne, arrived at La Trappe. He was accompanied by Marshal Bellefonds, Lords Dunbarton and Douglas, his confessor, Father Sanders, and some others. The Abbot did not think the presence of royalty justified any departure from the ordinary menu of the guest-quarters, so the visitors had to be content with eggs and vegetables ; neither fish nor flesh was offered them. Next morning the King assisted in the sanctuary at the High Mass. At the beginning of the Gospel he unsheathed his sword and held it aloft in his right hand until the deacon had finished : this was the custom of the English Sovereigns since the time when Henry VIII received from the Pope the title *Defensor Fidei*. He received Holy Communion, kneeling on the second

step of the altar, and heard a low Mass in thanksgiving.

The whole party dined with the monks in the
common refectory, where everything went on just
as usual. After dinner James expressed a wish to
see a religious who, from a desire of even greater
solitude than the monastery afforded, lived alone in
a poor hermitage some distance away in the heart
of a forest. He had once been a very distinguished
soldier, and was known as Marquis de Nocey. In
reply to the Monarch's queries, he said that he
attended Mass every morning in the monastery
church at half-past three. " Nonsense !" exclaimed
Lord Douglas, " you don't mean to tell us, surely,
that you can make your way in the darkness of
night through such a tangle of briers and brush-
wood. And how would you manage in rain or
snow ?" The old soldier smiled. " I have faced
and surmounted greater difficulties than that," he
answered, " in the service of an earthly king :
would it not, then, be a shame to shrink from the
hardships, very light in comparison, which I
encounter in the service of the King of heaven ?"
" Quite right," said James, " it is indeed a disgrace
that men will do almost anything for an earthly
sovereign and almost nothing for the Sovereign of
the universe."

Before leaving next morning the King said to

De Rancé : " This monastery is the only place where one can learn to have due respect for God ; if He spares me, I hope to return soon and make a retreat with you." He then fell on his knees for the Abbot's blessing.

CHAPTER XX.

Letter to James II—The Duchess de Montbazan's Sisters—De Rancè again denounced as a Heretic —His Comments on Arnauld's Death—His Maladies — An Operation — Resignation — New Abbot of La Trappe dies—Dom Gervaise appointed his Successor.

AFTER his return to Saint-Germain, where he had taken up his residence, the throneless Monarch sent a letter to Abbot de Rancé requesting him to draw up a set of rules for the guidance of his conduct. The Abbot very willingly complied with this request. Helping souls was his business, his profession ; it made no matter whether it happened to be the soul of a prince that required his assistance or the soul of a peasant. The long epistle addressed to James concludes with the words :

" In short, Sire, God has willed in times past to prove to the world that sanctity is not incompatible with sovereign power. He has willed that the hands of saints should hold the sceptre. Hence we have the canonised kings : Henry, Louis, Edward, Edmond, and many others. You, Sire, are walking in their footsteps, and with such fidelity as to give ground for the hope that you will participate in the glory which is their reward, whether by the good use you will make of the authority, soon, as I hope, to be restored to you, or by your resignation to the designs of Providence, if it be God's will that you should purchase at the price of a limited and transitory greatness a greatness and a glory infinite in worth and everlasting in duration.''

James paid five more visits to La Trappe, making each time a retreat of three or four days, and joining in all the monastic exercises. He corresponded very frequently and very familiarly with the Abbot whom he revered as a saint. Eighteen letters addressed to him by De Rancé have been preserved. What follows is an extract from the Monarch's own memoirs :

'' Ever since it pleased the Divine Goodness to touch my heart with His powerful grace during my sojourn at La Trappe, I have been endeavouring with the assistance of the same grace to reform my life. It was partly out of curiosity I went to the monastery the first time. I wished to know if the description which had been given me of the holy place and the accounts I had read of it in England would correspond to my own personal impressions, and to see if the Abbot who had originated the reform there deserved all the praise bestowed upon him. One of my old friends, Marshal Bellefonds, insisted on my going thither, a service for which I can never be grateful enough. I found that the desire I already entertained of living in a worthier way grew gradually stronger. Several times I repeated my visit to the monastery, and on each occasion made a kind of retreat for three or four days. Indeed, I have done this every year since my return from Ireland, for which I thank God, as I perceive the practice has done me much benefit. It has given me a fuller conviction of the vanity of human greatness. I now feel persuaded that nothing ought to be so ardently desired as the love of God, and that every good Christian is under obligation to mortify himself, especially one so miserable as I, who have lived so many years in a state of habitual sin, until Thou, O my God, delivered me therefrom by chastising me in Thine infinite mercy."

James learned at La Trappe to put up a better fight against the world, the flesh, and the devil than he had made against William of Orange. But whilst all admired his piety during his sojourn in France, there were those who thought, and said too, that he would have consulted better for his honour and reputation had he remained to share the hardships and dangers of the gallant troops he left to fight his battles in Ireland.

Amongst the many persons of quality who entrusted the Abbot of La Trappe with the direction of their conscience, the five sisters of the ill-starred

Duchess of Montbazan merit particular mention. All of them had consecrated their early years to vanity and worldliness. Having returned to God after their sister's death, they atoned for the dissipation of their youth by devoting the rest of their lives to the constant practice of prayer and penance. One entered the Cistercian convent of Malnoüe where, being elected abbess, she introduced the Strict Observance under De Rancé's guidance. Another, the Countess de Vertus, lived the life of a saint in the world, and practised such austerities that the Abbot was obliged to caution her against excessive zeal. " Your weak health requires that you should moderate your bodily mortifications ; but there need be no limit to interior penance, I mean mortification of your desires.'' During the last twelve years of her life she suffered a veritable martyrdom, and from her bed of pain looked only to heaven and La Trappe for consolation. The thought of death terrified her. " Jesus Christ Himself," wrote the Abbot, " experienced this feeling of terror, and testified to the same for the consolation of such as you. But if you resemble Him in this emotion, you must try to resemble Him also in the confidence He felt, in His utter abandonment of Himself to His Father's Will, and in His acceptance of the chalice presented to Him.'' Many of those about her were imbued with Jansenistic ideas, and tried to dissuade her from frequent Communion. She asked

the Abbot's advice. " I cannot see what there is
to prevent you from approaching the Holy Table
as often as you have been accustomed to," he
answered. " Your sufferings and the seclusion in
which you live can be made a sufficient preparation." Later on, when her torments became
almost unsupportable, he sent her these beautiful
words : " In God's present dealings with you, He
displays His justice indeed, but not less His goodness. He shows Himself as a Judge, but also as a
kind Father ; and I'm sure His clemency makes a
deeper impression on your heart than the rigour
of His severity. Submit to His Will whatsoever it
may demand of you. His designs are full of justice
and mercy ; hence you ought to love them. And
you must regard the hand that is smiting you now
as the same that soon shall crown you. Whatever
the afflictions He may send you, they must not
make you forget that He loves you tenderly. Can
you doubt it, after receiving so many proofs of His
affection ? You may have as much sorrow as you
please for the past, provided your confidence in the
divine mercy increases in proportion. It is confidence that will open to you the kingdom of Jesus
Christ."

The Abbot's enemies often put his name to
forged documents in order to get him into trouble.
One of his foolish admirers thought he might do
the same with a view to his glorification. An

ecclesiastic of Paris got possession of a collection
of maxims derived from the works of De Rancé.
After adding considerably to the list, he obtained
permission from the authorities to have them
printed, declaring that he had the Abbot's consent.
The printing was almost finished when the Abbot
first heard about the matter. He protested vigorously, and denied that he had ever given his
sanction for the publication of the work, some of
which was not his own at all. But the ecclesiastic,
unwilling to admit the deception, endeavoured to
brazen it out. People did not know what to think.
The Archbishop of Paris sharply rebuked the Abbot
for his want of candour. However, the truth was
soon discovered, and De Rancé's honour fully
vindicated.

Not many months later a book appeared with the
title : *Guillaume de Saint-Amour, hérésiarcque,
resusscité in la Personne d'Armand-Jean de la
Trappe*. This William de Saint-Amour, a scholar
of the thirteenth century, had been the sworn
enemy of the Mendicant Orders, to which he denied
the right to teach or preach or exercise any kind
of ministry. His work : *De Periculis,* was condemned by the Holy See. The new assailant of De
Rancé affected to see some resemblance between
that work—a diatribe against the illustrious Orders
of SS. Francis and Dominic, and the *De la Sainteté*.
Of course, they have as little in common as the

Genesis of Moses and Euclid's Geometry. It was
not merely a very malicious but also a very stupid
attack.   Its author overreached himself, for his
accusations were so wildly extravagant that nobody
believed them. So prosper all slanderers !

Dr. Antoine Arnauld, the corypheus of Jansenism,
died on August 8th, 1694. On receiving the news,
De Rancé wrote to the Abbé Nicaise :

" So M. Arnauld is dead ! After clinging to life
as long as he could he was obliged at last to pay
the common debt of mortality ! Well, whatever
one may say of him, his departure will at all events
put an end to the controversy. His erudition and
his authority were a great asset to his party.
Happy the man who has no other end in life than
Jesus Christ, and who, putting away all that can
separate us from Him, attaches himself to his
Saviour so strongly that nothing can ever seduce
him !"

This letter fell into the hands of the celebrated
dramatist, Racine, who had strong leanings towards
Jansenism. The result was another tornado. Every
Jansenist resented what they considered an insult
to their chief. Arnauld's successor, Quesnel, wrote
a long commentary on the offending letter, in which
he entirely misrepresented the Abbot's meaning.
But even Quesnel did not stoop to the meanness
that characterises the comments of M. Bremond.
This critic, who can blow hot and cold as it suits

him. is shocked and scandalised beyond expression at the Abbot's heartless words. But let him read what St. Bernard wrote to Peter the Venerable after the death of the antipope, Anacletus, and he will perceive how mild in comparison is the language of De Rancé.

We think it worth while to mention a little incident which shows the Abbot's way of dealing with his opponents. A priest of the Congregation of St. Maur had written a book : *De la Connaissance de soimême,* in which he opposed many of the opinions defended by De Rancé. He had difficulty in getting the necessary licence to print the work : it was the Abbot of La Trappe who obtained it for him.[1]

In 1695 the community of La Trappe saw with concern a serious aggravation of the maladies which had long been threatening their beloved Abbot's life. He suffered from severe gastric pains, due partly to his rigorous fasting and coarse food, partly to a rupture he sustained some years earlier whilst working in the fields ; a racking cough gave him no rest night or day ; rheumatism made every movement a torment ; his legs and right arm were greatly swollen ; erysipelas attacked his face and rendered him for awhile unrecognisable ; and, most serious of all, insomnia refused him that respite from sorrow and suffering which kindly nature has

[1] Abbot De Rancé had a Mass celebrated every day at La Trappe for all his enemies and opponents.

ordained for the relief of the tired and afflicted. His right hand was so inflamed that he could not even sign his letters. It had been operated on before. A second operation became necessary. The surgeon stood aghast when he saw the state of the hand, all ulcerated and purulent to an incredible degree. Observing that the patient did not so much as wince at the first incision, he suspected some miracle of impassibility had removed all sense of pain, and went gaily forward with his work. " Have you no feeling at all in this arm?" he paused to ask. " Well, rather," responded the Abbot dryly, " but nothing to complain of."

Some time before this the Abbot of Citeaux and the General Chapter, learning of his condition, commanded him in virtue of holy obedience to moderate his austerities. He had now to submit to an order to retire to the infirmary and to eat flesh meat. To the unlucky religious who first brought him that food he said : " You shall have to answer for this before God, for you will be the cause of my dying impenitent."

Seeing that he would be unable for the future to take part in the common exercises, and to give his religious, as St. Benedict requires of all superiors, the instruction of his good example, he judged that he ought to remain no longer at the head of the community. So he wrote to the King a very touching letter in which he declared that, being incapacitated by his infirmities for discharging the duties of superior, and needing the little time which remained to him to prepare for death, he believed he was acting in accordance with God's Will in soliciting his Majesty's permission to resign.

Louis granted the request. And he showed himself so propitious that De Rancé ventured to make a further petition. The monastery of La Trappe, according to arrangement, was again to have a commendatory abbot when the present incumbent went out of office. To safeguard the house in some degree against the ill-consequences of such a change, the Holy See had given the community the privilege to elect a prior who should be to a certain extent independent of the abbot. This expedient had many serious disadvantages, but it was the best that could be devised so long as the King insisted on his right to appoint a commendatory abbot. Emboldened by the kindness shown him, De Rancé begged Louis to forgo that right and to allow the appointment of a regular superior. The King consented. He even left the choice of a successor to De Rancé himself, who immediately nominated his prior, Father Zozimus.

Cardinals le Camus and de Janson busied themselves about procuring the papal Bulls for the new Abbot's installation. Pope Innocent XII gave them gratis, and in handing them to his friend, Cardinal de Janson, said : '' It is not so much at your solicitation I grant them, but on account of the great regard I entertain for the former Abbot of La Trappe.''[2]   Abbot Zozimus was installed on December 28th, 1695, and received the abbatial benediction on January 22nd of the year following. The community totalled at this time about one hundred persons in all, the choir and the lay religious being practically equal in number. They were not given much time to benefit by the direction of the new superior, for on March 3rd, less than three months after his installation, he went to his account. Everybody, but De Rancé in particular, mourned his loss as a real calamity. He had manifested all the qualities requisite in a religious superior, and enjoyed the fullest confidence of his brethren who regarded him as a saint, and not without cause.

King Louis again authorised De Rancé to choose an abbot for La Trappe. The man of his choice this time was Father Armand-François Gervaise, who had been a Discalced Carmelite and won a high reputation for piety, eloquence, and learning. Bossuet strongly recommended him for the abbatial office; it was indeed his recommendation that

---

[2] The Holy Father replied to the Abbot's letter through Cardinal Spada in the following terms : " The great merit of your paternity has won the Sovereign Pontiff's love and admiration to such a degree that he prizes your letter to him as a present of the utmost value and as testimony of your loyalty and devotion to his person. He is particularly pleased to learn with what zeal and assiduity you and your religious commend his interests to God."

decided De Rancé. Nevertheless the choice was not a happy one, as we shall see. Dom Gervaise showed his appreciation of the Reformer of La Trappe in a letter written after his appointment : " Alas for me ! What light, what virtue do I not stand in need of so as to become a worthy successor of so great and so holy a man, and to maintain the blessed reform which he has established in this monastery ! "

CHAPTER XXI.

Death of the Duchess de Guise—De Rancé painted—Semiquietism—Fenelon writes to the Reformer—Abbot Gervaise in Trouble—He resigns—De Rancé's Attestation—Monsieur Maisne—New Publications.

ON March 17th, 1696, the pious Duchess de Guise, cousin-german to Louis XIV, breathed her last. For twenty-five years she had been under the spiritual direction of Abbot de Rancé and her conduct during all that period testified to the prudence of her guide. After her death some of the instructions he had given her were published under the title : *Conduite Chrétienne addressée à Son Altesse Royale Mme de Guise par le Révérend Père ancien abbé de la Trappe.* Here is one piece of advice he gave her. Whenever any new project suggested itself to her mind, she should ask herself the question : *Quid hoc ad aeternitatem?* How does this look in the light of eternity ?

The Duke de Saint-Simon succeeded to his title in 1694 at the age of nineteen. Disappointed in his hopes of a suitable marriage, to console himself he made a retreat the same year in the monastery

267

of La Trappe. He conceived such an affection for De Rancé, that he could hardly speak of anything else. La Trappe saw a great deal of him thereafter : people looked upon him as the spoiled child of the holy Abbot with whom he made himself completely at home. Nor would he permit a word against De Rancé to be spoken in his presence. Once when driving with the Dukes de Charost, Beauvilliers, and Chevreuse, his companions, infected with Quietism, began to criticise the Reformer of La Trappe. " Gentlemen," said De Saint-Simon, " it would ill become a young man like me to ask you to stop this uncharitable conversation, but a man may jump out of a carriage at any age." On another occasion the Duke de Charost taunted him with his extravagant veneration for his " grandfather," as he called the Abbot. " You also have a grandfather," answered De Saint-Simon, " and the difference between yours and mine is this, that mine has never yet been justly found fault with."

The Duke de Saint-Simon had one great ambition—to have a portrait painted of his friend. But how was this object to be attained ? The Abbot had consistently refused to sit for the many artists who offered him their professional services. Two of these had presented themselves at the monastery as postulants, hoping for an opportunity of sketching him whilst he was celebrating Mass ! The plot being discovered, the " postulants " lost no time in getting back to Paris. Some medals bearing his image were going about; one had for device the words : *Rediva per illum Thebais,* another : *Restaurator vitae monasticae.* There were some paintings also, but very defective. De Saint-Simon wanted a real portrait, and he thought of a plan. He came to La Trappe one fine day accompanied by a gentleman who had an ardent desire to see and hear the Abbot de Rancé. When the latter appeared, the Duke told him that his friend, an officer, would listen to the conversation with pleasure, but would take no part in it, because, poor fellow, he stammered in a most awful way. The visitors had three long interviews with De Rancé. Sometimes he seemed to grow suspicious, when he found the silent officer eyeing him with a degree of attention which the occasion did not appear to warrant. However, he said nothing. The stammering " officer " was the celebrated portraitist Rigaud. After each séance he used to hasten to his room and record his impressions. The print that forms the frontispiece of this volume has been taken from his work. No other portrait has any claim to be considered authentic.

In 1696 Abbot de Rancé published in two volumes accounts of the lives and deaths of twenty-one members of his community. In the same year he became entangled in another and very bitter controversy through the indiscretion of his friend,

Bossuet. François de la Mothe-Fenelon, the gentle and pious Archbishop of Cambrai, adopted and defended a modified form of Quietism called sometimes Semiquietism, in his book entitled : *Explication des Maximes des Saints*. The work was immediately attacked by the Eagle of Meaux. The great Bishop found an opponent worthy of his steel in Fenelon who had many sympathisers amongst the upper classes. A copy of the *Explication* fell into De Rancé's hands. Having read it, he wrote to Bossuet :

" I have just read the Archbishop of Cambrai's book. It is incomprehensible to me how a man of his character can permit himself to be seduced by foolish fancies, opposed alike to Scripture and ecclesiastical tradition. I had thought that this system no longer found acceptance anywhere, that it only survived in the memory of those who grieved for having adopted it ; but I was mistaken. We know that you have employed your pen against this monstrous teaching. We know, therefore, that it has been demolished. For everything you write, Monseigneur, is accepted as a dogmatic decision. . . . . But whilst the Archbishop's book arouses my indignation, I pray Our Lord to enlighten him so that he may recognise and correct his errors. You, Monseigneur, have been chosen by God from amongst all men to be in our time the defender of truth. In all encounters hitherto you have maintained its interests with such success as makes it impossible to doubt the issue of the present conflict.''

A little later, acknowledging Bossuet's work, *Les Etats d'Oraison,* he wrote :

'' In truth, should these fanatics succeed in establishing their chimerical doctrines it would be necessary to burn the Holy Scriptures inspired of God, and the life and teaching of Jesus Christ would lose all their significance. There is a thoroughgoing impiety concealed under that extravagant and affected language which they employ for no other object save to seduce unwary souls. We shall pray God to touch their hearts and to enlighten their minds and to render them so docile that they will profit by the instructions you give them, either to abjure the error they have already embraced or to recognise what attracts them as the subversion of all Christian faith.''

Bossuet was so delighted to get such encouragement in a really tough fight that he could not refrain from showing the letters, meant to be strictly private, to his friends. He even allowed them to be published. Thus was the poor invalid of La Trappe dragged once more into the maelstrom. The friends of Fenelon poured all the phials of their anger on his devoted head ; he had to face a perfect cataract of abuse. But the Archbishop himself, although deeply pained at the

Abbot's language, made no expostulation. When he had read the letters he only remarked : '' I am truly unfortunate in being condemned by a man whom I esteem so highly. Why did he not address these letters to myself?'' He then sent the Abbot a copy of another of his works, the *Instruction Pastorale*, accompanied with a letter so modest and humble that no one can read it, remembering who and what the writer was, without being touched. But it is only in keeping with all we know of Fenelon.

'' I take the liberty, Monsieur,'' he began, '' to send you an *Instruction Pastorale* which I have written to explain certain passages in my book, *Des Maximes*. This explanation appears to me very necessary, for I see by your published letters that even one so enlightened and experienced as you has taken my words in a sense quite contrary to what I intended. It does not surprise me, Monsieur, that you have credited what has been told you to my disparagement with regard both to the past and the present. I am a stranger to you, and there is nothing about me that would render incredible any evil which men may ascribe to me. You have but borrowed your impression from a prelate deservedly renowned for his wisdom and learning. It is true, Monsieur, that if you had done me the honour of writing to me concerning the statements in my book which scandalised you, I would have either explained the offending passages or corrected

them. And should you have the kindness to send me
your opinion after reading my *Instruction Pastorale,*
I shall be quite ready, Monsieur, to profit by your
lights and to defer to your authority. Nothing you
have said against me has in the least altered the
sentiments of admiration I am bound to entertain
for your person and your work ; and I feel assured
that you will no longer condemn the doctrine of
disinterested love, when it has been cleared of the
obscurities in which my critics have involved it, and
when you understand that I have no sympathy with
such as would dispense with the hope and desire
of happiness in God. My teaching thereon is the
teaching of St. Bernard. He bequeathed it as a
most precious legacy to his children. And were
the sentiment and practice of pure love lost to the
world, it is in La Trappe we should expect to
recover them. . . . I cannot close this letter without
entreating your prayers and those of your community ; I need them badly. You, Monsieur, love
the Church ; so do I ; God is my witness that I
desire to live only for her.''

It would be impossible to doubt the good faith of
one who writes like that. Fenelon's good faith has
never been doubted. Nevertheless, nothing can be
plainer than that his teaching on disinterested love
would lead by logical consequence to disastrous
results. It was not by mere inference De Rancé
learned the evils of Quietism ; he had had very

sad experience of them in the case of a religious superioress whom the doctrine of disinterested charity plunged into the most frightful disorders, whence by the grace of God he at last succeeded in delivering her. If he replied to Fenelon, no trace of the letter has been found. But he refused to take any further part against the humble Archbishop of Cambrai.

The Abbot published a volume of Christian maxims —*Maximes Chretiennes*—in 1697, which greatly enhanced his reputation. Each pithy saying, *tum copia tum brevitate admirabilis,* contains matter enough for a long meditation. Here are some specimens :

" The highest object of our ambition should be a happy death, since we live only to die."

" Considered in the light of eternity, human greatness is but an obstacle to happiness."

" It is much better to speak to God than to speak of God."

" He who amasses the goods of this world only fortifies the walls of his prison."

" Virtue is like a tree : the more violently it is buffeted by the winds of temptation the more deeply it strikes its roots."

" Smother calumny under the weight of your good actions."

" Flattery can be of use by teaching us what we ought to be."

" We must never under any circumstances do what is evil, but it is sometimes the part of virtue to omit what is good."

" To preserve innocence one must believe oneself capable of committing all the sins one has not committed."

" Ordinarily those have the least pride who appear to have the most of it."

Abbot Gervaise, meantime, was learning in the hard school of experience that elevation in rank does not always imply immunity from trouble. As canonical visitor of the convent of Clairets, he ventured to alter some of the regulations introduced or approved by De Rancé. This excited the indignation of the good nuns who revered the old Abbot as a saint. Some of them, having high connections, brought the matter under the notice of the King. The result was a sharp reprimand from his Majesty to the unfortunate Gervaise. Louis gave him to understand very clearly that he must walk in the footsteps of his great predecessor, and must not presume to change anything either in La Trappe or outside it that had been established by De Rancé. The latter wrote at once to assure the King that he had no fault to find with the administration of his successor, and that nothing had been changed in the regime established at La Trappe. Louis declared himself satisfied. Not long afterwards Cardinal de Bouillon, French ambassador at

Rome, who had a niece in the community of Clairets, complained that Dom Gervaise put undue restrictions on the liberty of the nuns with regard to choice of confessors. Further difficulties with the same community determined him to renounce his jurisdiction over the convent altogether. This gave rise to new complaints, and the King ordered the Bishops of Seez and Chartres to investigate the matter.

Deaths occurred very frequently at La Trappe, and epidemics often visited the monastery. Abbot Gervaise attributed this mainly to the unwholesome situation of the house, encompassed as it was with stagnant pools and sombre forests. He decided to secure another establishment somewhere in the neighbourhood with more salubrious surroundings which would serve as a convalescent home for the sick of the community. De Rancé tried to dissuade him from the project, but in vain. Providence seemed to favour the design, for less than thirty miles from La Trappe, in an ideal environment for a sanatorium, was found an abandoned monastery, called Estrées, which could be purchased on easy terms. Dom Gervaise bought the property, and sent six religious to take possession, without waiting for the royal consent. This brought another reprimand from the King, with a command to recall the monks from Estrées.

Even the charity of his friends became a source

of embarrassment for the unfortunate Abbot. Being summoned to prepare the Bishop of Seez for death, and to draw up his last will, he found that the prelate intended to bequeath to La Trappe his silver plate and the precious ornaments of his private chapel. He protested as strongly as he could, representing that acceptance of such objects would be a violation of poverty, and besides would bring odium upon the community. The Bishop insisted : if the monks did not wish to retain the articles they could dispose of them as they pleased. To make sure his intentions would be carried out, he had the plate and ornaments sent to the monastery before he expired. The result more than justified the Abbot's presentiment. Such an outcry was raised against the monks of La Trappe by the Bishop's relatives that the property had to be restored. At the same time the report spread abroad that the new Abbot was treating his predecessor with unheard of cruelty, and aimed at substituting the Carmelite observance in La Trappe for that hitherto followed there.

Crushed and despairing under the weight of such an accumulation of troubles, Dom Gervaise could see only one course open to him. He handed in his resignation. The community petitioned the King not to accept it. De Rancé wrote a separate letter in which he acknowledged that the Abbot had taken the wisest course, yet requested that he should be kept in office until the times should be more favourable. Later on, seeing discord entering the community, he advised the immediate acceptance of the resignation. But as to the reports in circulation that he was ill-treated personally, and his reform undone by Dom Gervaise, he made this solemn declaration :

" I, Brother Armand-Jean, formerly Abbot of La Trappe, recognise and, under present circumstances, feel it my duty to declare that my successor, the Reverend Dom Armand-Francois, has been blessed with such success in the government of this community that never has piety been more fervent or observance more exact. I recognise and declare that all the established penitential and disciplinary practices have been preserved and maintained so ardently and zealously that visitors coming here see nothing but what edifies them. This happy condition of things must be regarded as a result not only of the Abbot's instructions, but also of his prayers and good example.

" I feel also obliged to testify that almost from the hour of his installation his personal character and reputation have been made the objects of attack, and that many false charges have been alleged against him. I, who am always present in the monastery, have never witnessed the misconduct he is accused of. This I certify to be the truth.

" I testify further that I have not words strong

enough to reprobate the outrageous malice of his maligners. It has been reported that he never addresses me except in an offensive manner, that he cruelly reproaches me, as if his purpose was to cause me pain and annoyance, and that not long ago he went so far in his abuse that I said I could not stand it any longer and intended to look for peace of mind in some other monastery. I declare before God and men that there is not a word of truth in these rumours. On the contrary, whenever Dom Gervaise comes to see me, he invariably goes down on his knees, as if he were a novice and I the superior, and despite my best endeavours I have hardly ever succeeded in persuading him to rise. Never have I heard from his lips, in all my conversations with him, a single word that could possibly be regarded as opposed to charity, propriety or good sense. That is saying too little. I have never heard anything from his lips which was otherwise than becoming for him to speak and for me to hear. I mean all I have here said to be taken literally, as perfectly true in every detail.

" Given at La Trappe, this 17th day of October, 1698."

Then the secretary's pathetic subscript : "Taken down from the dictation of the Very Rev. Father who can neither write nor sign his name on account of the paralysis of his right hand.—Maisne."

All the senior members of the community subscribed the above attestation with the formula :—

" We, the senior religious of the abbey of La Trappe, subscribe to the above attestation, as being ocular witnesses of what is there asserted."

But however irreproachable (so far) the personal character of Dom Gervaise, and however wise his administration, the prejudice against him outside the monastery was so general and violent that his continuance in office could only injure La Trappe. So his resignation was accepted, and Father de la Cour was appointed in his place.

Dom Gervaise, unhappily, had not virtue enough to support the humiliation of his fall. After giving a good deal of trouble and not a little scandal, he quitted La Trappe for another house of the Order, and spent the remainder of his life migrating from one monastery to another. He held Monsieur Maisne, Abbot de Rancé's secretary, responsible for all his misfortunes. This gentleman entered La Trappe as an oblate, that is, he undertook to remain until death in the monastery, and to be faithful to all the observances, without taking vows. As he was expert in the use of the pen and had a reputation for prudence, De Rancé employed him as his secretary. He became much attached to his saintly master. There can be no doubt that he was mainly responsible for the reports spread abroad of the cruel conduct of Dom

Gervaise towards the Reformer; Maisne disliked
Gervaise quite as much as he loved De Rancé.
Neither can there be any doubt that such reports
were absolutely groundless. Whether the secretary's
conduct must be attributed to malice or misunderstanding is a question impossible to decide. At all
events, Dom Gervaise had good cause to feel
aggrieved. But when he asks us to believe that
Maisne intimidated Abbot de Rancé to such an
extent that the latter trembled before him, he offers
an insult to our common-sense. The man who
could stand up to Sovereign Pontiffs and hurl
defiance in the face of despots like Mazarin, would
hardly tremble in presence of such a poor creature
as Maisne. De Rancé treated all men with respect
and charity, but he kept his trembling for God
alone.

In his indictment of De Rancé, M. Bremond
makes a capital point of the undeniable fact that
for many years the Abbot employed as private
secretary this Monsieur Maisne, thus admitting a
layman with no religious obligations and little sense
of responsibility into the conscience-secrets of the
countless souls whom he directed by correspondence. The charge appears formidable enough. But
it loses much of its force when the circumstances
are considered. In the first place, everybody knew
the position occupied by Maisne at La Trappe, so
that the Abbot's correspondents could always take

it for granted that whatever they put on paper
would come to the knowledge of the lay secretary.
If, in spite of this, they exposed in their letters their
troubles of conscience we fail to see why he should
be censured therefor, particularly as he never invited
but rather discouraged such confidences.

But, says our critic, Maisne was utterly unworthy of the delicate position he held, and the
Abbot had the responsibility of putting and keeping
him there. De Rancé, of course, may have been
guilty of an error of judgment : greater than he
have made such mistakes. But there can be no
doubt that the Abbot had the utmost confidence in
his secretary's discretion and loyalty. Nor was he
the only person who implicity trusted Maisne.
Even Bremond himself admits that many fine ladies
not only sought spiritual direction from the Abbot
through the secretary, but actually made manifestation of conscience to the secretary himself ! The
idea of a layman acting as spiritual director did not
appear so strange to the faithful of the seventeenth
century as it appears to us. We know that at least
one lay contemporary of M. Maisne, D'Andilly
Arnauld, did quite a brisk trade as director at Port
Royal.

But why did not De Rancé choose a professed
member of his community for this responsible and
difficult office ? He has told us the reason himself,
but Bremond refuses to believe him. A monk's

duty is to follow the exercises prescribed in the Holy Rule of St Benedict, and to " prefer nothing to the work of God," that is, to attendance in choir. So the Abbot did not think it right to ask any of his religious to give up these occupations— the privileges to which their profession entitled them —for the routine work of the secretariate.

With regard to Bremond's statement that the secretary became the actual ruler of La Trappe : this is one of the many, many instances where the learned Academician has managed to confound the illusions of his imagination with objective fact.

This year (1698) Abbot de Rancé published a work entitled : *Conférences ou Instructions sur les Epîtres et les Evangiles des Dimanches.* The conferences represented the discourses he had preached in chapter on Sundays and Holidays, which according to Cistercian custom, were longer and more elaborate than the instructions given on week days. Like all his other publications, they abound in striking images and epigrammatic expressions. Speaking of the limitations of human power, he employs a homely illustration very similar to that of a modern writer—viz., that the monarch who governs half the world is unable to do so small a thing as to stop a sneeze. " Learn to work out your salvation with fear and trembling," he says to religious, " for it would be a dreadful misfortune to miss the goods of heaven after sacrificing, in

order to gain them, the goods of earth : to lose at
once both God and the world.'' And describing
the monk who leaves the cloister, he uses this
comparison : '' Watch a river as it courses across
an extensive plain. So long as it remains in its
bed and between its banks, it bears on its bosom a
multitude of barques heavy-laden with the mer-
chandise, the provisions, and the various other
commodities which give prosperity and abundance
to all the towns and districts where it passes. But
should it chance to make a breach in the embank-
ment which confines its waters, then it abandons
its natural bed, leaving it dry and arid. It flows
with impetuosity about the fields, it tears up the
soil, it sweeps away trees and crops, it covers the
hitherto fertile land with sand and stones, and
converts it into a dreary waste. And when it
returns to its ordinary channel, it brings back with
it all the foulness and stench of the fields it has
flooded.'' The person who fosters self-will is
compared to the fool who throws open the cage of
a man-eating lion.

The following year, 1699, witnessed the publication of De Rancé's *Reflexions morales sur les
quatre Evangiles,* in four volumes. We might call
this work, *The Gospels Meditated*. That title will
sufficiently explain its character. Another book
from the pen of the same author saw the light a
few months later. This was the *Traité des Obliga-*

tions des Chrêtiens. He composed it at the urgent request of his friends, Cardinal le Camus and Bishop de Barillon, who desired him to do for those whose lot is cast in the world what he had already done so admirably for religious persons in his work : *De la Sainteté et des Devoirs de la Vie Monastique.* It was his last literary production, the Benjamin of his genius, and it showed that, despite his cruel bodily sufferings, his imagination still retained all its verve and his intellect all its vigour. The *Journal des Savants,* in its issue for November 16th, 1699, said of the book : " Although this subject has been treated already by a countless number of authors, perhaps never before have its various aspects been presented with so much clarity, so much solidity, such beauty of diction and style, as in the present work."

CHAPTER XXII.

De Rancé's last days—His Death—Grief of the Community.

THE Reformer's prolonged martyrdom was now visibly drawing to a close. No one ever heard from his lips the least word of complaint—unless it be considered a complaint to repeat the prayer of St. Philip Neri: *Adauge, Domine, dolorem sed et adauge patientiam.* "O Lord," he wrote, "I should need a thousand hearts to feel all the gratitude I owe Thee for the compassion Thou hast taken on my misery. What better proofs of Thy mercy could I possibly have than those Thou hast given me? Or what surer and more efficacious means to close my wounds, to cure the various evils and maladies with which it has pleased Thee to chastise Thy servant at the end of his days? I do not ask Thee to soften or diminish the pains which rack my body, but only for an increase of patience. I only ask Thee not to suffer me to be guilty in my torments of any movement, any word, sign or action, which would be out of accord with the grateful submission Thou hast a right to expect. Let me appeal to Thy clemency in the words of the Prophet : ' Cast me not off in the time of my old age ' (Ps. lxx, 9).'' '' Here,'' says Dubois, '' every phrase is a sob of anguish, every word a tear : that page appears to have been written with the blood that escaped from his wounded hand.''

Evidently the Lord heard his prayer for patience. '' By the grace of God I feel quite resigned,'' he said, '' but I am so far from suffering these trifling afflictions with the dispositions of the saints that I fear I shall derive no merit from them.'' Only the involuntary twitching of his face revealed the torments he endured. He never spoke of his ailments, except to make light of them, and he always wore a bright and serene expression. His courtly manners, the envy and despair of his worldly friends, never left him. And he would treat the last of the lay brothers with the same politeness as he would manifest towards the noblest of the land. He seemed to forget his own sufferings in his sympathy for others. Being no longer able to walk unaided, he had himself carried to the bedside of other patients where he would sit consoling them as only he knew how, although it was evident that the effort of speaking cost him pain. All the sweetness in his nature was brought to the surface in the crucible of affliction, '' not in the least altering his native character,'' says the distinguished writer, René Bazin, '' but only tempering its impetuosity.'' Whilst he governed the community he had exhibited all the qualities of a wise and affectionate father : he showed himself more like a mother now.

What a day was his ! Regularly at 2 a.m. he was taken from his hard bed and put sitting on his poor straw chair. There he remained immovable until 7 a.m., when he was helped to the church for Mass and Holy Communion. Then back again to his chair. His food consisted of two ounces of bread each day and a few spoonfuls of broth : even this he could not take without experiencing bitter anguish. And nevertheless whilst in such a state of suffering as might be expected to absorb all the energies of his mind, he daily dictated brilliant compositions to his secretary, M. Maisne.

We have spoken in an earlier chapter of the gift De Rancé possessed for assisting souls in their death-struggle. He had exercised it generously and successfully even whilst he lived in the world. Needless to say, he had not lost it in the cloister. Of all the religious who died in La Trappe since he came there, hardly one fought the last decisive fight without him : the last object visible to their darkening sight was the face of their beloved Abbot, the last sound that filled their ears was the whispering of his familiar voice.

And what death-scenes he witnessed ! Most frequently it was the happy consummation of a life passed in innocence, the serene sunset of a beautiful summer's day. But sometimes it was the going home of the repentant prodigal—sunshine after storm. Nothing in monastic history surpasses in beauty and interest Abbot de Rancé's account of the four Palemons who succeeded one another in La Trappe. First of the name was Chevalier des Essars, once famous as a duellist, who died in the odour of sanctity. The next was Nicholas des Haies, who in the world had led a life of scandalous disorders. When he beheld the bed of ashes on which, according to rule, he was to die, he exclaimed in rapture : " I cannot say, like St. Andrew : ' O good cross, long and ardently desired !' But I will say : O blessed couch, for which I have longed and sighed these many years !" Paul d'Harchies, formerly a captain of dragoons and a confirmed infidel, then inherited the name. The fourth Palemon, Count de Santena, had been the greatest sinner of all, which is saying much. He came to La Trappe to see d'Harchies whom he had known in the army. He saw him, but stretched on the bier, for he arrived on the day of his friend's death. After the funeral, which deeply impressed him, whilst kneeling before the altar, he asked God, like Saul, to show him what he should do. Immediately the well-known voice of d'Harchies sounded in his ears, saying : " Remain in this monastery and take my name and place." He did as he was told, and spent the rest of his days in the practice of heroic virtue. Then there was the ex-grenadier, Brother Muce, whose life and death in religion were as virtuous as his early career had been vicious. The last prodigal to go to heaven from the monastery, assisted in his agony, like the others, by De Rancé, was the young Scottish nobleman, Robert Graham, who died in 1699, at the age of twenty-three. His father, a colonel in the army of King James, and his mother were both bigoted Protestants. Robert became a Catholic in boyhood, but abandoned his faith later on to please his mother, and ended by abandoning all Christian faith and morality. By his prayers during his three years at La Trappe he had the happiness of bringing both his parents into the one ark of salvation.

It was thus Abbot de Rancé spent his time in the infirmary, inspiring the sick with patience and the dying with confidence. The religious sometimes saw him on his knees beside the layer of ashes whereon the expiring monk was laid, with the blood streaming from his wounds, re-opened by his efforts, forgetful of his pains, forgetful of everything except the urgent need of his spiritual child. " On such occasions," writes Dubois, " he resembled the general of an army, who, wounded himself unto death, raises himself laboriously from the ground, and leaning on his broken sword, encourages his troops to continue the fight for the honour of their king and country."

At last he who had assisted so many others to die received the dread summons himself. At the beginning of October, 1700, his condition became so serious that death seemed to be imminent. His throat, tongue, gums and palate became ulcerated, and he began to suffer from a violent fever. To the brother infirmarian who expressed his grief at seeing him in so sad a state he replied : " Brother, we must adore the divine ordinances with humble sub-mission. And surely it is about time my career came to a close." The cellarer came weeping to receive his last admonitions : " We must all part," said the poor sufferer. " Be faithful to God and to the promises you have made Him and He will never abandon you. Love the good Father Abbot whom Heaven has given you, as he loves you." Then, making the sign of the cross on his visitor's forehead, he said simply : " Pray to the Lord for me."

Death did not come as soon as expected. The patient lingered on in frightful suffering until the 27th of the month. During that interval, the famous Jansenist " saint " and wonder-worker, Mademoi-selle d'Almayras, better known as Sœur Rose, came to the monastery to offer him her services as a miraculous healer. The Duke de Saint-Simon, who ungenerously describes the lady as alarmingly ugly, tells us that she was credited with miracles, ecstasies and visions ; and she certainly lived a life of extraordinary austerity. Even Bossuet himself speaks of her miraculous cures. De Rancé absolutely refused to have anything to do with her. " I have no desire to be cured," he said, " and, even if I had, I should not dream of employing a remedy so suspicious." Sœur Rose left La Trappe a disappointed woman.

On the morning of October 26th Mass was celebrated in the sufferer's cell, and he received Holy Viaticum with the devotion of a Seraph. Although every movement of his ulcerated tongue must have caused him severe pain, he was constantly making aspirations, his favourites being : *Christe Salvator mundi, miserere mei ; Tibi soli peccavi ; Cor mundum crea in me, Deus, et spiritum rectum innova in visceribus meis ; Adoramus Te, Christe, et benedicimus Tibi, quia per sanctum crucem Tuam redemisti mundum.* Another ejaculation often heard from him was this : *Domine, Domine, episcopis miserere.* On the same day (26th) he who had once been known as Brigadier de Saint-Louis told him that he should be very happy and very confident going to God, considering the wonderful fervour and peace that reigned in the community he had governed. " It is God Who has done all," was the reply. " And so far from attributing any credit to myself, I am sincerely convinced that any other, given the same graces, would have made a better use of them. Still, I am not without confidence that God in His goodness will pardon me all my offences." He spent the day as usual, sitting on his straw chair, recited the whole Office, and even dictated a few letters. In the afternoon the Sacrament of Extreme Unction was administered. After the ceremony, seeing the religious on their knees around his bed, he assured them that he had always borne the heart and the affection of a father for each one of them, that their sanctification had been the single purpose of his life, and that he would never forget them. Somebody asked where he would like to be buried. "In the most desolate and abandoned spot on earth," he answered.

In the evening Mgr. d'Aquin, Bishop of Seez, arrived to give the dying man a parting blessing. De Rancé yearned to see also his life-long friend, the Bishop of Meaux. But Bossuet, to his infinite regret, found it impossible to make the journey. When the Reformer saw Mgr. d'Aquin at his bedside, he took his hand and made with it the sign of the cross on his forehead, then kissed it. "You see, Monseigneur," he whispered, "how God is pleased to manifest the riches of His goodness towards me in all the different circumstances of my life. He has constantly showered His graces upon me with infinite liberality, but I have not known how to put them to profit. I have answered His beneficence only with ingratitude and infidelity.

Yet, in spite of all, you see how He continues to favour me with an abundance of graces and blessings." When the Bishop asked if he still felt all his old affection for the children God had given him, he answered : "Monseigneur, for several years now I have been but a simple religious in the community, just like the others. They are no longer my children, but my brothers in Christ. I am assured of their love and of the benefit of their prayers. And if it were permitted me to regret the loss of my voice, I should grieve at my inability to tell them how dear they are to me and with what tenderness I enclose them all in the centre of my heart. It is my hope to keep them there and to present them before the Lord, if He vouchsafes to receive me into the bosom of His mercy."

That night, Abbot de Rancé made a general confession to the Bishop with such humility and compunction that the latter was deeply moved. Before withdrawing, the prelate asked if he had any last message for the King : "I beg you," he said, "to assure his Majesty of my loyalty to his sacred person. If it should please God to admit me into heaven, I shall not cease to pray for his sanctification and for the prosperity of the State. I entreat his Majesty to continue to protect the monastery of La Trappe and to maintain the strict discipline established therein. This is the last humble petition which I take the liberty to present to him." As soon as the Bishop retired, Abbot de la Cour entered the cell accompanied by a few of the religious. Seeing him, De Rancé exclaimed : " Reverend Father, I love you, I honour you. Do not forget me in your prayers, and I shall never forget you in the presence of God ; for although I am only a wretched sinner, I have confidence, nevertheless, that of His goodness He will deal mercifully with me." De la Cour declared that he had a special claim to the prayers of his predecessor, since he had sacrificed himself for him by taking on his shoulders the burden of the administration. To which the dying man replied : " God never withdraws His protection from those superiors who have accepted their office only at His command, and who have no other aim but His glory and the salvation of souls. Rest assured, Reverend Father, that He will bless you. And as for me, I shall never cease to pray for all your wants." He then requested his superior to make his excuses to King James ; he had begun a letter to the Monarch, but had been unable to finish it. As the reader will soon discover, James himself was not then far off from the close of his earthly career.

At 2 a.m. next morning he had himself taken out of bed, as usual, and placed in his chair. Abbot de la Cour asked if he would like to see once more the whole community before he went to heaven. " It would make me very happy," he answered.

So they came to receive his last blessing with sorrow in their hearts and tears in their eyes. After exhorting them in his failing voice to preserve inviolate the virtues of peace and fraternal charity, he said : '' I pray Our Lord to bless you and to protect you under the shadow of His wings, to pour His choicest graces upon you and to make you monks according to His own Heart. I entreat Him to maintain you in the concord and charity in which you now live. Charity is the virtue that will conduct you to Paradise. By it you will abide in Christ and Christ in you, and it will make you one with Him for all eternity. That is the happiness I desire for you, in the name of the Father, and of the Son, and of the Holy Ghost. Amen. Continue to practise all your observances without alteration or diminution, for they have been inspired by the Spirit of God. Be you all for Jesus Christ as He is all for you. Be so faithful to Him that nothing shall ever be able to make you displease Him in the least thing.'' Then extending his arms towards them he cried in a firm voice : '' Adieu ! May Jesus be with you all for ever.''

Mgr. d'Aquin returned at 5 a.m. Having said something to De Rancé about making a sacrifice of his life to God, he received the answer : '' Alas, Monseigneur, what is my life and what am I that you should speak thus ? I neither have nor am anything worthy of being offered in sacrifice to the

Divine Majesty." After a pause the sufferer added : " By God's grace I am so disposed as to be equally willing to continue in pain or to pass out of life, according as He shall ordain. I ask Him for the grace to have no other will but His at all times and in every thing." He was then heard to exclaim : " O eternity ! What happiness, O my God, to be with Thee for all eternity !" Noticing the brother-infirmarian kiss the feet of a crucifix, he said : "Brother, you should also kiss the death's head. For it is death that puts an end to our exile and all our miseries ; death is the door by which we go to Jesus Christ."

In the afternoon, when it became evident that he had not many moments to live, he was laid on the bed of ashes whereon he had seen so many others expire. Mgr. d'Aquin knelt on the floor at his side, and held his hand whilst the prayers for the agonising were recited. The prayers finished, the Bishop said to the dying man : " Do you ask pardon of God ?" "Monseigneur," came the whispered reply, " with all humility, and from the bottom of my heart I pray God to pardon my sins, howsoever heinous and numerous they may be. I tremble before His justice, but at the same time, through His grace, I feel as much confidence as a child in the goodness of his father. I conjure the Father Almighty, the Father of mercies, and the God of all consolation, through the merits of the Blood of Jesus Christ, to receive me into the number of those who shall sing His praises and rejoice in His love for evermore." The Bishop began to recite some verses from the Psalms, to which De Rancé feebly responded.

Thus, the Bishop: " The Lord is my light and my salvation."

De Rancé : " Whom shall I fear ?"

The Bishop : " If a battle shall rise up against me."

De Rancé : " In Him shall I place my confidence."

The Bishop : " Thou, O Lord, art my Helper and my Protector."

De Rancé—making a violent effort : " O my God, do not delay."

These words were his last. He gently pressed the Bishop's hand, as if in farewell, looked at him affectionately, turned his eyes, full of love, on the religious weeping around him, and then fell asleep in the Lord. He died at 1.30 p.m., October 27th, 1700, in the seventy-fifth year of his age, and the thirty-seventh of his life in the cloister. The weary body could rest at last, the wounded heart would ache no longer. Having faithfully " borne the burden of the day and the heats," the labourer had been summoned home where God shall wipe all tears from our eyes, " and death shall be no more, nor mourning, nor crying, nor sorrow shall be any more, for the former things are passed away."

Two hours after death, the body was borne to the community church and placed on the bier before the High Altar. The religious noticed with astonishment that the face of the deceased, which during the last few years of his life had been so pale and haggard, appeared now full and ruddy, and wore a peaceful expression in which there was something suggestive of majesty. Next day, the feast of the Apostles Simon and Jude, from 3 a.m. until noon Masses were said without interruption for the repose of his soul; for besides the priests of the community, the secular clergy of the neighbourhood came in crowds to offer in his behalf the Sacrifice of expiation. As for the religious, overwhelmed with inexpressible grief, they could find no consolation anywhere except on their knees beside the holy body. They kissed his hands and feet, they pressed their faces against his, they applied their rosary beads to the cold and rigid flesh as if to give them a new consecration, and all the while the tears flowed in torrents from their eyes. We have all this from the testimony of an eye witness, the sub-prior, Father le Nain. In a letter to a friend the same religious writes:

" How shall I express myself? The light of the Cistercian Order has been extinguished here on earth, but only to shine eternally in heaven. . . . . I cannot describe to you the greatness of my grief, the utter desolation in which his loss has left me.

No one ever, not excepting father or mother or my brother Tillemont, has occupied such a place in my heart as my beloved Father Abbot. I was bound to him by the closest ties that can be formed by grace and nature ; and the thirty-three years I have lived with him have rendered those ties so strong that nothing but God's almighty power can break them. Break them, have I said ? No, they shall never be broken. They shall endure throughout the whole of eternity."

No, Monsieur Bremond, heartless tyrants are not so loved ; not so loved are humbugs and hypocrites.

The interment took place on the 29th, after the Solemn High Mass of Requiem, sung by Mgr. d'Aquin. The chant was almost drowned amidst the sobs and lamentations which the orphaned community made hardly an effort to suppress. People regarded it as a remarkable coincidence that at the moment when the uncoffined body was being lowered into the grave the choir happened to be singing these verses of the 131st Psalm :

" If thy children shall keep my covenant and these my testimonies which I shall teach them

" Their children also for evermore shall sit upon thy throne.

" For the Lord hath chosen Sion : He hath chosen it for His dwelling.

" This is my rest for ever and ever ; here will I dwell for I have chosen it."

According to the ancient custom of the Order, abbots should be buried in the chapter house. But it was Abbot de Rancé's dying request to be laid to rest in the cemetery amongst his brethren. Such a petition could not, of course, be refused. As the religious loved to pray at his graveside, they asked the Abbot to have the place covered in, so that the inclemency of the weather should not be able to prevent them from satisfying their devotion. For this purpose, a small chapel was erected over the grave some years after the burial. The body being exhumed on that occasion was found well preserved and exhaled not the faintest hint of an offensive odour. Reverend hands placed it in a leaden coffin and over it built a beautiful monument on the table of which was carved a recumbent figure of the Reformer.

The following is a copy of the mortuary notice sent to all the houses of the Order, according to custom, after the great Abbot's death : —

Anno Dom. 1700, *die* 27 *Octobr., in monast. de Trappa Strictioris Observantiae Cist. Ord., dioeces. Sagiensis, sacramentis Ecclesiae rite munitus, in sacco et cinere humi jacens, filios suos ad poenitentiae perseverentiam exhortans, expiravit admodum reverendus Pater Domnus Armandus Joan.*

Le Bouthillier de Rancé, ejusdem coenobii abbas, anno aetatis suae 75, conversionis 37, praesente Illust. et Rev. D. Sagiensi episcopo. Pro cujus animae refrigerio vestras orationes precamur ex charitate, et orabimus pro vestris.

Anima cujus per Dei misericordiam requiescat in pace. Amen.

CHAPTER XXIII.

Testimonies to De Rancé's Greatness—Biographies.

WE shall here cite some of the eulogies pronounced on Abbot de Rancé after his death by persons eminent in Church and State. After receiving the news of his friend's departure, Bossuet wrote : — " Although it is saddening news that I have lost so dear a friend, I thank you for your thoughtfulness in letting me know it without delay. . . . . This only can I say of the beloved dead : he was another St. Bernard in learning, in piety, in mortification, in humility, in zeal, in penitence ; and posterity will rank him amongst the reformers of monastic life. He will have received a great welcome from the multitude of religious whom he has sent to heaven before him."

Abbot Gourdan of Sainte-Genevieve expressed his feelings thus : —

" My heart is pierced with sorrow at the news. It is not merely the light of the Cistercian Order that has been extinguished, but the light of the Universal Church—*Extinctum est lumen Israel.* Armand-Jean de Rancé was another Elias, another

Baptist. . . . . For myself, who have known him these twenty-eight years, I can say that I have never had a truer friend in this world. I will add without any exaggeration that, after God, no one has been so much the object of my love as he. In truth, the very thought of him has always been a source of joy to my heart. I have found consolation in talking about him and in reflecting on God's admirable providence over him ; and I have esteemed it a happiness to have been considered worthy of a participation in his solicitude, in the charity of his prayers, and the wisdom of his counsels. I have no doubt he holds an eminent place in Paradise, so that I almost fear to pray for him lest I should seem to detract from his merits. May God be praised for giving us so illustrious an example of sanctity ! May the discipline he established endure for ever, and be transmitted intact and inviolate from generation to generation !''

Father de la Chaise, S.J., confessor to Louis XIV, wrote to Abbot de la Cour of La Trappe : —

'' No one can appreciate better than I the greatness of the loss you have suffered by the death of your saintly Abbot. The example of his virtuous life will bear fruit for many a year not alone in your holy community, but throughout the entire Christian world. His Majesty, to whom I have given an account of his death, so precious in the sight of the Lord, has been deeply touched. The more faithful your community are in walking in the footsteps of your pious reformer and observing the rules established by him, the more pleasing will they become to God and the more a source of edification to His Church."

The Grand Duke of Tuscany sent the following letter to the bereaved community : —

" Your Abbot *emeritus* has crowned by a happy death a life wholly beautiful, wholly consecrated to God. This great servant of the Divine Majesty, who has been justly called the edification of the Universal Church, enjoys now in heaven the recompense due to his labours. So long as I live I shall not cease to remember his holy life with sentiments of veneration. It is my hope that the charity he showed for his neighbour whilst he still lived amongst us will inspire him in heaven, where he now is, to obtain from the Most High the pardon of all my sins."

" At Fontainebleau," writes the Duke de Saint-Simon in his *Memoirs*, " I received one of the greatest shocks of my life when I heard that I had lost my friend, the Abbot de Rancé. One day, when I was awaiting the King, the Bishop of Troyes showed me a letter announcing that the Abbot was at the point of death. My first impulse was to speed off at once to La Trappe. I was dissuaded from so foolish a proceeding by the counsels of my friends. . . . . These *Memoirs* are too profane to insert an account of a life of such sublime sanctity or of a death so noble and precious in the sight of the Lord. Therefore, I shall content myself with saying here that the Abbot was honoured with many splendid and elaborate eulogies, and that the King himself pronounced his panegyric in public. People from all parts of Europe appear to vie with one another in manifesting their appreciation of so great a loss."

Our next testimony is from King James II :—

" I have been much surprised and affected," he wrote to Abbot de la Cour, " by the tidings that your holy Abbot has gone to receive his reward. And yet, considering the state of his health for a number of years past, the news should not have found me unprepared. Always ' precious in the sight of the Lord is the death of His saints,' and there can be no doubt that Abbot de Rancé's death may be so described. Like all others who have had the happiness to know him, I have lost a powerful support by the departure of that holy religious. I can never sufficiently acknowledge my obligations to him for having aroused me from the lethargy wherein I lay, just as the majority of those who are obliged by their state to live in the world, and where in spite of my misfortunes I, like the rest, permitted myself to be made the sport of passion. Had I not persevered in following the good advice of this holy Abbot, God only knows what would have become of me. Lord Perth, at his arrival here, placed in my hands the relics of my saintly friend which you had the kindness to send me. They are a treasure I prize very dearly and shall never part with. I know not how to thank you for so precious a gift.

" I have no intention to give up my custom of visiting La Trappe after Easter. Even though my love for you were not strong enough to draw me thither, I should go, nevertheless, out of love for myself ; because I feel that my sojourns in your holy solitude fortify and encourage me in the state wherein I am placed and wherein God keeps me. I have need of such examples as your monastery affords."

At the end of this very humble letter from the fallen Monarch, his Queen, Mary of Modena, added the following : " The King allows me to tell you here that I am infinitely grateful for the crucifix and the book you have sent me as relics of your holy Abbot. You could not possibly have given me greater satisfaction than by offering me these gifts, so dear and venerable. I received intelligence of Abbot de Rancé's holy death with mixed emotions of joy and sorrow which it is impossible to describe, but which, as I think, you will comprehend. For it seems to me that you yourself, and all who were privileged to know the saintly religious must have experienced the same sentiments. I was delighted to hear from Lord Perth that, although you have lost your beloved father, his spirit still lives in the community and in the heart of each of its members. I pray God with all the fervour of my soul to keep you constantly faithful to the guidance of that spirit, for His own greater glory and the edification of the whole world. For my part, I assure you that I shall always feel a profound veneration for your monastery and a very particular esteem for a person who has been chosen by a saint to be placed at the head of a holy community.''

King James had not the opportunity of making many more visits to La Trappe, as his career came to a close on September 16th, 1701. From his dying bed he sent a message through Lord Perth to Abbot de la Cour and his community, telling them that on the frontiers of eternity he wished to acknowledge all he owed to La Trappe, where he had received so many divine favours, and in particular to Abbot de Rancé whose holy counsels had put him and kept him in the way of peace and salvation ; it was to the edifying examples he had witnessed in that monastery, he declared, should be attributed the Christian sentiments that now filled his heart, and the grace of complete resignation. A graceful gesture this, and characteristic too ; for James, if not always a saint, had been always a gentleman. He died like a true Christian, happy in the thought that he had gained more at La Trappe than he had lost at the Boyne.

Of the esteem in which the holy Abbot was held during his lifetime by the most eminent personages of the day, the reader has already had evidence. Three Popes, Alexander VII, Innocent XI, and Innocent XII, treated him with distinguished honour. All the papal nuncios who represented the Holy See at the French court during his life at La Trappe—Ranucci, Nicolini, Delfini, and Gualteri—testified their admiration for his virtue and character. Numbers of cardinals, both French and Italian, and practically all the bishops of France were proud to call themselves his friends. '' Our bishops,'' writes Le Nain, '' entertained so high an esteem for him that they used to consult him on the most important matters of business,'' and several of them put themselves under his spiritual direction. We have seen with what respect he was regarded by the Sovereign Princes Louis XIII, Louis XIV, James II, and the Grand Duke of Tuscany. Littérateurs and philosophers like Nicaise, Baluze, Leibnitz, Santeuil, Malebranche, Fleury, Pellison, the Duke de Saint-Simon, Madame de la Fayette, and Ménage, loved and revered him.

Ménage, in his *Menagiana,* an appreciation of the celebrities of his time, writes of De Rancé : " I never read the works of the Abbot of La Trappe except with admiration. His style is noble, sublime, inimitable. His erudition is always profound, his reasoning subtle, his intellect superior, his life irreproachable : and the reform he has established is the work of God. One can say of him what Philemon said of Zeno : he has made hunger popular.

Several Popes of later times have expressed in one way or another their appreciation of Abbot de Rancé and his work. Benedict XIII accepted the dedication of an Italian *Life* of the illustrious Reformer. Clement XII patronised in the same way an Italian translation of his great work, *De la Sainteté*. Pius VI more than once eulogised him. In his Bull elevating the monastery of Port-du-Salut to the dignity of an abbey, Pius VII declared that he wished the religious " to live according to the rules of the reform established by the venerable Abbot, Armand-Jean le Bouthillier de Rancé, rules which have merited the commendation of our predecessors, the Sovereign Pontiffs Innocent XI, Benedict XIV, and Pius VI, and which we also by these presents approve and confirm." Pius IX, in a decree dated February 25th, 1847, made honourable reference to " Armand-Jean le Bouthillier de Rancé, who re-established the discipline practised in the time of St. Bernard, and who, to consolidate his reform, drew up a code of wise constitutions which have deserved to be eulogised by the Holy See." Nor has our present Holy Father disdained to add his voice to this chorus of praise. In approving the Revised Constitutions of the Order of Cistercians of the Strict Observance, January 26th, 1925, he wrote : " Wherefore, in this, as formerly in other religious families deriving their origin and their rule from St. Benedict, God raised up and inspired holy men to labour for the restoration of the primitive observance. Amongst such reforms of monastic discipline, especially memorable is that which took place during the seventeenth century in the abbey of La Trappe, an abbey which has belonged to the Cistercians since the time of Pope Eugenius III. This reform rendered the Trappists famous throughout the world."

We might go on indefinitely citing such testimonies to the holiness and greatness of the Reformer of La Trappe. But we shall close the list with the following appreciation taken from the preface to the first edition of the Cistercian Regulations published after the French Revolution by the authority of the General Chapter. It will show in what esteem Abbot de Rancé is held in the Order :

" The labours and trials of this great man of God form one of the most beautiful pages of monastic history. They resulted in securing for La Trappe a new importance. Our gratitude will never permit us to forget him ; it shall always equal our admiration.''

The first biography of Abbot de Rancé appeared two years after his death, that is, in 1702. Its author, the Abbé Maupeou, was a secular priest, curé of Nonancourt in the diocese of Evreux. He showed that he had neither the knowledge nor the judgment required for the undertaking, and his two volumes rather injured than honoured his hero. The year following, Canon Marsallier, who had already published biographies of Cardinal Ximenes, Henry VII of England, and St. Francis de Sales, gave the world a new *Life* of De Rancé. He spoiled his work by a deliberate effort to represent the holy Abbot as a sympathiser with Jansenism. The book aroused great indignation at La Trappe, and was interdicted in most houses of the Order. Bossuet also complained of it. The great Bishop suggested that Father le Nain, who had lived in most intimate associations with the Reformer for thirty-three years, and therefore could speak of him with special authority, should compose a new *Life*. This work appeared posthumously in 1715 in three large volumes, reduced later on to two, and bore the title : *La Vie du R. P. Dom. Armand-Jean le Bouthillier de Rancé, Abbé et Réformateur de la Trappe*. The author, following too literally the advice of Bossuet, passed over in silence all the controversies in which De Rancé had been engaged, and thus detracted seriously from the historical value of his work. In 1744 Dom Gervaise published his *Jugement Critique, mais équitable des Vies de feu M. l'Abbé de Rancé*, which contains much valuable information omitted from the earlier biographies ; for the *Jugement* is itself a biography. An Italian *Life* appeared in 1706, which was soon superseded by another entitled : *Vita di D. Armando Giovanni le Bouthillier de Rancé, abate regolare et riformatore della Trappa.* This was dedicated to Pope Benedict XIII. Friedrich Maurer brought out a German *Life* in 1820 : *Leben des Dom Armand Johanns le Bouthillier de Rancé, Abts und Reformators des Klosters la Trappe.* Next came the *Life* by Chateaubriand, which the illustrious author wrote in obedience to his confessor. Whatever may be thought of this as a literary production, it has not very much merit from the historical point of view. In 1866 the Abbé Dubois published his *Histoire de l'Abbé de Rancé et de sa Reform,* in two volumes, which despite its prolixity, merits to be considered as the standard biography of the great Abbot. Finally, we have Albert Cherel's *Rancé,* issued 1930, with a splendid Introduction from the pen of the celebrated writer, Renê Bazin. We have not included the *Abbe Tempête* in the list of biographies and

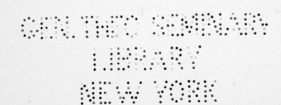

studies of De Rancé, because it is neither a biography nor a study, nor yet a combination of both. It belongs to a class apart, and tells us much more about M. Bremond than about the Reformer of La Trappe. We had intended to describe it as a brilliant lampoon, but having read G. K.'s review of the work in the *Universe,* we shall defer to his better judgment and content ourselves with describing it as '' a brilliant squib.''

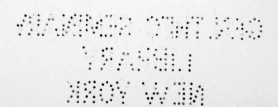